ABC, My Grannie Caught a Flea

My Grannie Caught a Flea

SCOTS CHILDREN'S SONGS AND RHYMES

Ewan McVicar

BIRLINN

First published in 2011 by
Birlinn Limited
West Newington House
10 Newington Road
Edinburgh
EH9 1QS

www.birlinn.co.uk

ISBN: 978 1 84158 937 4

British Library Cataloguing-in-
Publication Data
A catalogue record for this book
is available from the British Library

Designed and typeset by
Mark Blackadder

Printed and bound in the UK by the MPG Books Group

Contents

Introduction

Scotland is rich in many things, not least in our traditional children's songs and rhymes. Every Scots child and adult can sing 'Ally bally bee' and 'Ye canny shove yer grannie'. The other small rhythmic words we use to comfort or amuse very small people, and the vigorous games and funny rhymes we recall from playground days, will vary according to our age and where we were brought up. Older people lament that the young 'don't sing in the playground any more', but school playtimes are hotching with song and rhyme.

True, few of the pieces popular 40 years ago can be found in action today. The kids casually make new rhymes from snatches of TV commercials and popular song. They remake – and sometimes mangle – old pieces, and ruthlessly discard most that are fondly remembered by adults, but this has always been the case. Look into collections in books and archives – you will find thousands of childhood rhymes and songs that flourished, then faded away.

This book celebrates the richness of those older sources, combined with the fruits of the author's visits to Scottish schools from 1991 to 2006. The songs and rhymes are rich in vigour and bounce, direct language, the Scots voice, humour, observations on adult relationships that are sometimes sharp and sometimes naive, and surreal imagery.

As you read them, you will half recognise old favourites but often say, 'Those are the wrong words' because they are not what was used in your street or playground. Elements were trimmed off, shuffled, recombined, pruned, turned into nonsense, then into a new form of sense. I have included varying versions of a few to show how they grow and decline.

What are they for? For the children, amusement and to accompany physical activity, of course, but also for practising, developing and showing off language skills. For adults, fond memories of simpler times?

Sittin On Yer Mammie's Knee

Though few readers of this book were raised in a nursery, the term 'nursery rhyme' is usually attached to songs and rhymes that adults use when hushing and calming, manipulating and entertaining and developing language knowledge of babies and very small children. 'Baloo' was a favourite old Scots term for a lullaby, and our lullabies can be simple croons or wordy small songs. The rhymes to accompany 'teaching' body parts, bouncing, clapping and tickling are direct and rhythmic.

HUSHABAWS, BALOOS AND LULLABIES

For rocking the baby

Baloo lillie beetie
Mammie's at the creetie
For tae plick an tae pu
For tae gather lammie's woo
For tae buy a bullie's skin
Tae rock wir bonnie bairnie in
Orkney, Gossett, 1915

Baloo ma peerie lamb
Cuddle close to mammie
Mammie'll sing a bonny song
Ba ma prettie lambie
Orkney, 1961, SSS

Bonnie Jean o Fogieloan, she langed for a baby
She took her father's grey cat and rowed it in a plaidie
'Hishie bishie bow row, lang leggies ow ow
And twerna for your hairie mouthie
    I wad kiss you now now'
Aberchirder, 1905, GD

Now balaloo lammy, now baloo my dear
Now balaloo lammy, ain mammie is here
What ails my wee bairnie? What ails it this night?
What ails my wee lammy? Is bairnie no right?
Now balaloo lammy, now baloo my dear
Does wee lammy ken that its daddie's no here?
Ye're rockin' fu sweetly on mammie's warm knee
But daddy's a-rockin upon the saut sea
Moffat, 1933

Hurr hurr dee noo, hurr hurr dee noo
Noo faa dee ower, my lammie
Hurr hurr dee noo, hurr hurr dee noo
Dere nane sall get my lammie
Hurr dee, hurr dee, mammie sall keep dee
Hurr dee, hurr dee, mammie is here
Shetland, Hendry & Stephen, 1982

Hush ye, hush ye, little pet ye
Hush ye, hush ye, dinna fret ye
The Black Douglas sall not get ye
Fraser, 1975

Hush-a-ba baby, lie doon
Your mammie's awa tae the toon
And when she comes back, ye'll get a wee drap
Hush-a-ba baby, lie doon
Aberdeenshire, 1908, GD

Hushie-ba, Burdie Beeton
Your mammie's gane to Seaton
For to buy a lammie's skin
To wrap your bonnie boukie in
Chambers, 1842

BALOO BALILLI

Baloo balilli, baloo balilli
Baloo balilli, baloo ba

Gae awa, peerie fairies, gae awa, peerie fairies
Gae awa, peerie fairies, fae oor bairn noo

Dan come boanie angels, dan come boanie angels
Dan come boanie angels ta wir peerie bairn

Dey'll sheen ower da cradle, dey'll sheen ower da cradle
Dey'll sheen ower da cradle, o wir peerie bairn
Shetland, Buchan, 1962

CAN YE SEW CUSHIONS?

O, can ye sew cushions and can ye sew sheets?
And can ye sing Bal-lu-loo, when the bairn greets?
And hee and ba birdie, and hee and ba lamb
And hee and ba birdie, my bonnie wee lamb

Hee o, wee o, what would I do wi you?
Black's the life that I lead wi you
Owre mony o you, little for to gie you
Hee o, wee o, what would I do wi you?
Chambers, 1842

HEY DAN DILLY DOW

Hey dan dilly dow, how den dan
Rich were your mither, gin ye were a man
Ye'd hunt and ye'd hawk, and keep her in game
And water your father's horse in the mill dam

Hey dan dilly dow, how den flowers
Ye'll lie in your bed till eleven hours
If at eleven hours ye list to rise
Ye'll get your dinner dicht in a new guise
Laverock's leg and titlin's tae
And aa sic dainties my mannie sall hae
Herd, 1776

Hushaba Babie

Hushaba, babie, lie still, lie still
Your mammie's awa to the mill, the mill
Babie is greeting for want of good keeping
Hushaba babie, lie still, lie still

Hushaba, babie, lie still and sleep
It grieves me richt sairly tae hear ye weep
Hee and ba lilliloo, down dilly dan
Sing hee and ba, birdie, my bonnie lamb
Moffat, 1933

Hush-A-Ba Birdie

Hush-a-ba birdie, croon, croon
Hush-a-ba birdie, croon
The sheep are gane to the silver wood
And the coos are gane to the broom, broom

An it's braw milking the kye, kye
An it's braw milking the kye
The birds are singing, the bells are ringing
The wild deer come galloping by, by

Hush-a-ba birdie, croon, croon
Hush-a-ba birdie, croon
The gaits are gane to the mountain hie
And they'll no be hame till noon, noon
Chambers, 1842

CHIN CHAPPIE MOU MERRY

Face-tracing — fingers climb
over the baby's head

Chin chappie
Mou merry
Nose nappie
Cheek cherry
Ee winkie
Broo brinkie
Ower the hills and awa
Forfar, 1948

Come ower the hillie
Chap at the doorie
Keek in
Lift the sneck
Dicht yer feet
And walk in
Forfar, 1948

I'll tell you a story
Aboot Johnnie Norry
He gaed up twa stairs
And in at a wee doory
MacLennan, 1909

Here's the broo o knowledge
Here's the ee o licht
Here's the bubbly ocean
Here's the pen knife
Here's the shouther o mutton
Here's the briest o fat
Here's the vinegar bottle
And here's the mustard caup
Forfar, Rymour, 1911

DANCE TAE YER DADDY

For bouncing the baby

Dis is da wey da dogs gaed ta da hill
Aff a knowe and on a knowe
Dis is da wey da cats gaed ta da mill
Hame ageen, hame ageen, spinnin spinnin
Shetland, Saxby, 1932

Tea's in the pot, sugar in the cup
Hi, Buckie Willie, is your rhubarb up?
Dundee, Wellington, 1950s

The bairn in the cradle, playin wi the keys
Tammy i the kailpot up tae the knees
Pussy at the fireside, sappin aa the brose
Doon fell a cinder an burnt pussy's nose
MacLennan, 1909

The lady goes to market
Trit trit trit
The gentleman goes to market
Trot trot trot
But the farmer goes to market
Trit-trot, trit-trot, trit-trot
Dingwall, 1940s

Up, Chicki Naigie, buy white breid
Tell the King the Cardinal's deid
Dunbar, Rymouth, 1919

DANCE TO YER DADDIE

Dance to your daddie, my bonnie laddie
Dance to your daddie, my bonnie lamb
Ye'll get a fishie, on a little dishie
Ye'll get a fishie, when the boat comes hame

Dance to your daddie, my bonnie laddie
Dance to your daddie, my bonnie lamb
Ye'll get a coatie, and a pair o breekies
An a furly-giggie, an a souple Tam

Dance to your daddie, my bonnie laddie
Dance to your daddie, my bonnie lamb
An ye'll get a slicie o a dishie nicey
An a sweetie wiggie, an a mutton ham
Chambers, 1842 and Rymour, 1928

FEETIKEN FATIKEN

For manipulating fingers and toes and feet

Dis peerie grice gaed tae market
Dis peerie grice stayed at hame
Dis peerie grice hed meat tae ate
And dis peerie grice hed nane
And dis peerie grice
Said, 'Wee wee wee wa aa the wye hame'
Shetland, 1961, SSS

John Smith, fellow fine
Can you shoe this horse o mine?
Yes sir, and that I can
As weel as ony man
There's a nail upon the tae
To gar the pony speel the brae
There's a nail upon the heel
To gar the pony pace weel
There's a nail, and there's a brod
There's a horsie weel shod
Chambers, 1842

Peedie Peedie
Paddy Luddy
Lady Whisle
Lodey Whusle
Great Odomonclod
North Ronaldsay, Hendry & Stephen, 1982

There was Tam o my back, an Tam i my lap
An Tam o my knee, an Tam sookin me
Tam fiddler, Tam piper, Tam wi the gleyt ee
Tam here, Tam there, Tam o the lea
Aberdeenshire, 1910, GD

There's ma mither's knives and forks
There's ma mither's table
There's ma sister's looking glass
And there's the baby's cradle
Rock, rock, bubbly-jock
Gies a piece an tracle
Lossiemouth, 2006

This is the man that brak the barn
This is the man that stealt the corn
This is the man that run awa
This is the man that tell't aa
And puir Pirly Winkie paid for aa
Chambers, 1842

Thumb bold
Thibity-thold
Langman
Lickpan
Mamma's little man
Hendry & Stephen, 1982

Wag a fit, wag a fit, whan wilt thou gang?
Lantern days when they grow lang
Harrows will hap and plougs will bang
And every auld wife tak the tether by the tap
And worry worry worry till her heid fa in her lap
Dumfriesshire, Rymour, 1928

What will we row his wee feetie in
His wee feetie in, his wee feetie in?
What will we row his wee feetie in
In the cauld nights o winter?
Row them in a rabbit-skin
A rabbit-skin, a rabbit-skin
Row them in a rabbit-skin
In the cauld nights o winter
Glasgow, 1957, SSS

CLAPA CLAPA

Clapping with, tickling and prodding the baby

Ba birdie in a bog
Doon amang a pickle fog
Ba birdie ran awa
An I socht him aa day
And I fand him oot at last
Hidin in a craw's nest
An I took him by the powe
An I flang him owre the knowe
An tell'd him to rin hame
Cauld, wat an hungry wean
MacLennan, 1909

Clap clap handies
Mammy's awa tee wall
Daddy's awa workin
For a new shawl
Forfar, 1948

Clap clap handies
Mammie's wee wee ain
Clap clap handies
Daddie's comin hame
Hame till his wee bonnie
Wee bit laddie
Clap clap handies
Hendry & Stephen, 1978

Clapa clapa handies, daddie's comin hame
Pennies in his pocket for a good wee wean
West Lothian, 1990s

Clap-a-clap-a-handies
Mammie's at the well
Daddie's away to London
To buy wee baby a bell
Edinburgh, Ritchie, 1965

Dingle dingle gowd bow
Up the water in a low
Far up i Ettrick
There was a waddin
Twa and twa pikin a bane
But I gat ane, my leefu-lane
Deuk's dub afore the door
There fell I
Aa the lave cried, 'Waly waly'
But I cried, 'Feigh, fye'
Perthshire, Chambers, 1842

Heat a wummle, heat it weel
Bore it into Geordie's creel
Rymour, 1911

I ken something, I'll not tell
All the birdies in the town cam to ring the bell
Argyllshire, 1901

Poussikie poussikie wow
Where'll we get banes to chow?
We'll up the bog, and worry a hogg
And then we'll get banes enow
Chambers, 1842

There was a man i Muir o Skene
He had dirks, and I had nane
But I fell till'm wi my thoombs
And wat ye hoo I dirkit him, dirkit him, dirkit him
Rymour, 1911

I Maun Hae Ma Goun Made

It's I hae gotten a braw new goun
The colour o the moudiwort
I bade the tailyer mak it weel
An pit linin i the body o't
I bade the tailyer mak it weel
An pit linin i the body o't

I maun hae my goun made
Goun made, goun made
I maun hae my goun made
Like ony bigger lady

Side an wide aboot the tail
Side an wide aboot the tail
Side an wide aboot the tail
An jimp for my body
Rymour, 1928

Twa Wee Dogs

Twa wee dogs gaed awa tae the mill
Tae fecht aboot a lick o meal
The tane got a lick an the tither got nane
An the twa wee dogs cam toddlin hame
Calder Ironworks, 1860s

Twa peerie dogs, gaein to the mill
Trill trill trill
Tak a lick oot o this man's pock
An tak a lick oot the next man's pock
An tak a lick oot o tither man's pock
An hame again, hame again
Wiggly waggly, fill fill fill
Stenness, Orkney, 1961, SSS

The Golden City

Singing games

This section shares only games that are distinctively Scottish; others you may remember include 'Bobby Bingo', 'The farmer's in his den', 'Nuts in May', 'Tisket a tasket', 'When I was a lady' and many more, but these were, and are, played in much the same way throughout Britain and abroad. The games here often have puzzling language elements, but while we do not know what was meant by the 'merry matanzie' or the 'jingo ring', we do know that 'Babbity Bowster' derives from an older game called 'Bab at the bowster' and that Cocky Bendie was a small, bumptious person. Some of the games were for play-courting, others for movement, dance and procession.

You may find here some favourites I include later as activity songs, as I can see no clear line that divides game from activity.

A Gypsy Came A-Riding

A gypsy came a-riding
A-riding, a-riding
A gypsy came a-riding
Ipsy dipsy doo dah

What you riding here for?

Came here to marry

Who're you gonny marry?

I'm gonny marry four-eyes

Who the heck is four-eyes?

Her first name is Caroline

How you gonny get her?

Climb through the keyhole

Stuff it up with bubble gum

Climb through the windows

Lock all the windows

Climb down the chimney

Put a big fire there

[Spoken] Then I'll blow your house down
[Spoken] *Well, you can have her*
Glenrothes, 1981, SSS

Apples and Pears

Apples and pears, they make you six
They make my heart beat twenty-six

Not because they're dirty, not because they're clean
Not because they kissed a boy behind a magazine

Hey girls, do you wanna have fun?
Here comes Eve with her knickers on fire

She can dae the wibble wobble, she can dae the splits
But I bet you ten bucks that she can't do this

Just close your eyes and count to ten
If you mess up, just do it again
Culbokie, 2006

Apple on a stick will make me sick
Will make my heart go 2 4 6

Hey boy, do you want a fight?
Not because you're dirty, not because you're clean
Not because you kissed me behind the old scene

You can walk, you can talk, you can do anything
Bet you can't do it with your eyes closed
Moray, 2006

BABBITY BOWSTER

Wha learned you to dance, Babbity Bowster,
    Babbity Bowster
Wha learned you to dance, Babbity Bowster brawly?

My minnie learned me to dance, Babbity Bowster,
    Babbity Bowster
My minnie learned me to dance, Babbity Bowster brawly

Wha ga'e you the keys to keep, Babbity Bowster,
    Babbity Bowster
Wha ga'e you the keys to keep, Babbity Bowster brawly?

Ma minnie ga'e me the keys to keep, Babbity Bowster,
    Babbity Bowster
Ma minnie ga'e me the keys to keep, Babbity Bowster
    brawly
Chambers, 1842

Bee baw babbity, babbity, babbity
Be baw babbity, babbity, bounce the ballie

Kneel down, kiss the ground, kiss the ground,
    kiss the ground
Kneel down, kiss the ground, kiss a bonnie wee lassie

I wouldn't have a laddie, o, a laddie, o, a laddie, o
I wouldn't have a laddie, o, I'd have a bonnie wee lassie

Choose, choose, who you'll take, who you'll take,
    who you'll take
Choose, choose, who you'll take, I'll take a
    bonnie wee lassie
Rymour, 1913

BAKIN BETSY BELL

And it's bakin Betsy Bell, cum a ree o, cum a raddie o
And it's bakin Betsy Bell, cum a ree o, cum a raddie o

And it's on wi the hammer and the block

And it's on wi the studdy and the stock

And it's on wi the kettle and the pan

Then it's on wi the poker and the tangs

Then it's on wi the waterin can

And it's on wi the red cowl man
Rymour, 1911

BONNY MAY

Bonny May, will ye come oot? Will ye come oot,
    will ye come oot?
Bonny May, will ye come oot and help us
    wi oor dancing?

Out o my sicht, ye dirty slut, your faither
    was a tinkler
He made a pair o shoon for me, they didna
    last a winter
Loanhead, Rymouth, 1840

GLASGOW SHIPS

Glasgow ships come sailing in
Come sailing in, come sailing in
Glasgow ships come sailing in
On a fine summer morning

You dare not stamp your foot upon
Your foot upon, your foot upon
You dare not stamp your foot upon
Or Gentle John will kiss you

Three times kiss you
Four times kiss you
Send a piece of butter and bread
Upon a silver saucer

Who shall we send it to?
Send it to, send it to
Who shall we send it to?
To [Mrs McKay's] daughter

She washes her face, she combs her hair
She leaves her lad at the foot of the stair
She wears a gold ring and a velvet string
And she turns her back behind her
Argyllshire, 1901

Have You Ever?

Have you ever ever ever in your long-legged life
Seen a long-legged sailor with a long-legged wife
No, I've never never never in my long-legged life
Seen a long-legged sailor with a long-legged wife

Have you ever ever ever in your short-legged life
Seen a short-legged sailor with a short-legged wife

Have you ever ever ever in your knock-kneed life
Seen a knock-kneed sailor with a knock-kneed wife

Have you ever ever ever in your bow-legged life
Seen a bow-legged sailor with a bow-legged wife
Culbokie, 2006

How Many Miles to Babylon?

How many miles to Babylon?
Three score and ten
Will we be there by candlelight?
Yes, and back again
Open your gates and let us through
Not without a beck and a boo
There's a beck and there's a boo
Open your gates and let us go through
Chambers, 1842

King and queen of Cantelon
How many miles to Babylon?
Eight and eight, and other eight
Will I get there by candlelight?
If your horse be good and your spurs be bright
How mony men have ye?
Mae nor ye daur come and see
Chambers, 1842

I Sent a Letter to My Love

A drop-see a drop-see, a-dee a-doo a drop-see
I sent a letter to my love and by the way I lost it
I post it

I had a little dog, I sent for snuff
He broke the box, and skailed the snuff
He'll not bite you, nor you, but YOU
Helmsdale and Portgower, Rymour, 1919

Sea shells, cockle shells
Eevory ivory over
I wrote a letter to my love
And on the way I dropped it
I dropped it once, I dropped it twice
I dropped it three times over
Over over over
In and out the clover
Glasgow, 1960s/70s

I'll Give You a Paper of Pins

I'll gie you a pennyworth o preens
That's aye the way that love begins
If you'll walk with me, leddy, leddy
If you'll walk with me, leddy

I'll no hae your pennyworth o preens
That's no the way that love begins
And I'll no walk with you, with you
And I'll no walk with you

O Johnie, o Johnie, what can the matter be
That I love this leddy, and she loves na me?
And for her sake I must die, must die
And for her sake I must die
Chambers, 1842

I'll gie tae you a yalla hairy muff
Tae keep your handies warm when the
            weather's cauld and rough

I'll no hae yer yalla hairy muff
Tae keep ma handies warm when the
            weather's cauld and rough

I'll gie tae you a cosy armchair
Tae rest yoursel in when your
            beens are auld and sair

I'll no hae yer cosy armchair
Tae rest mysel in when ma
            beens are auld and sair
Aberdeen, Lomax, 1951

I'll gie you a dress o red
Aa stitched roon wi a silver thread
If you will marry, arry arry arry
If you will marry me

I'll no tak your dress o red
Aa stitched roon wi a silver thread
An I'll no marry, arry arry arry
An I'll no marry you

I'll gie you a silver spoon
Tae feed the wean in the afternoon
I'll no tak your silver spoon
Tae feed the wean in the afternoon

I'll gie you the keys o my chest
An aa the money that I possess
Yes, I'll tak the keys o yer chest
An aa the money that you possess

Oh ma Goad, ye're helluva funny
Ye dinna love me but ye love my money
An I'll no marry, arry arry arry
An I'll no marry you
Glasgow, 1950s

IN AND OUT THOSE DUSTY BLUEBELLS

In and out those dusty bluebells
In and out those dusty bluebells
In and out those dusty bluebells
I am the master

Tipper ipper apper on my shoulder
I am the master

Follow me my master says
I am the master
Rottenrow, Glasgow, 1960s/70s

KEEP THE SUNNY SIDE UP

Keep the sunny side up, up
And the other side too, too
See the soldiers marching along
And Paul McCartney singing a song

Bend down and touch your toes
Then you're an Eskimo

Bend down and touch your knees
Then you're a Japanese

Bend down and touch your hands
Then you're a Pakistan

Bend down and touch your chin
Then you're an Indian

Keep the sunny side, keep the sunny side
Keep the sunny side up
Cha cha cha!
Temple, Glasgow, 1960s/70s

LONDON BRIDGE

London Bridge is falling down
Dan's sister and Lady Ann
London Bridge is falling down
With a See, Si, So

We'll build it up wi penny buns
    The penny buns would be aa eaten up
We'll build it up wi silver and gold
    The silver and gold would be stolen awa
We'll get a wee man to watch it at nicht
    But if the wee man should fa asleep?
We'd get a wee dog to bark at his lug
Rymour, 1911

POOR MARY

Poor Mary lies a-weepin
Mary lies a-weepin, a-weepin, a-weepin
Mary lies a-weepin on sighs summer day

On the grass go she shall be
Till the grass grows on the field
Stand up stand up, polly veelly veep
And show me the girl and the next two asleep

How do you marry? I'd marry for joy
First to a girl, and the next to a boy
Garrynamonie, South Uist, Lomax, 1951

Queen Alexandra

Queen Alexandra has lost her gold ring
Send for the king, lost her gold ring
Queen Alexandra has lost her gold ring
Guess who has found it
Edinburgh, Ritchie, 1965

Round Apples

Round apples, round apples, by night and by day
The stars are a valley down yonder by day

The stars – poor Annie with a knife in her hand
You dare not touch her, or else she'll go mad

Her cheeks were like roses, but now they're like snow
Oh Annie, oh Annie, you're dying I know

I'll wash her with milk, and I'll dry her with silk
I'll write down her name with a gold pen and ink
Argyllshire, 1901

Sally Walker

Sally Sally Waters, sprinkling in a pan
Rise Sally, rise Sally, for a young man

Come choose from the east, come choose from the west
Come choose out the very one that you love the best
Now there's a couple married in joy
First a girl and then a boy

Now you're married you must obey
Every word your husband says
Take a kiss and walk away
And remember the promise you've made today
Fochabers, 1894

Rise, Sally Walker, rise if you can
Rise, Sally Walker, follow your gudeman

Come choose to the east, come choose to the west
Come choose to the very one that you love best
Now they're married I wish them joy
Every year a girl or boy
Loving each other like sister and brother
And so they may be kissed together

Cheese and bread for gentlemen
And corn and hay for horses
A cup of tea for aa good wives
And bonnie lads and lassies

When are we to meet again?
And when are we to marry?
Raffles up, and raffles down, and raffles aa a-dancin
The bonniest lassie that ever I saw was
    [*name of child in centre*] dancin
Aberdeen, 1894

SANDY SEATON'S WOOING

O Sandy Seaton's gane to woo
Down by Kirkady Lea
And there he met wi a puir auld man
His guid father to be

He led his daughter by the hand
His daughter ben brought he
'O, is not she the fairest lass
That's in great Christendye?'

'I winna marry wi ony lad
In aa the land o Fife
I winna leave my mammie yet
And I winna be his wife'

He's courted her and brocht her hame
His guid-wife for to be
He's gi'en her jewels and gi'en her gold
And he's kissed her three times three
Fife, 1933

The Galley, Galley Ship

Three times round goes the galley, galley ship
And three times round goes she
And three times round goes the galley, galley ship
Till we sank to the bottom of the sea

'Pull her up, pull her up,' cried the sailor boys
'Pull her up, pull her up,' cried he
'Pull her up, pull her up,' cried the sailor boys
Till we sank to the bottom of the sea

'No, I won't, no, I won't,' cried the sailor boys

'Yes, I will, yes, I will,' cried the sailor boys

Choose your neighbours, one or two
One or two, one or two
Choose your neighbours, one or two
Around the merry-ma-tanzie

Shake your tails till the bride comes in

A guinea-gold watch to tell her name

A treacle scone to tell his name

Now it's time to show your face
Edinburgh, Rymour, 1911

THE LONDON BALL

Up against the wall, the London ball
The London ball, the London ball
Up against the wall, the London ball
An a bonnie bunch o roses

Ah met ma laud in the bramble law
Wi a bonnie bunch o roses

Ha ha ha, ye needna rin
Wi a bonnie bunch o roses
Ma faither bocht a new top-coat
An Jeannie tore the lining
Ha ha ha, ye needna rin
For ye'll get yer licks in the morning
Leven, 1960, SSS

THE MERRY-MA-TANZIE

Here I gae round the jingie ring
The jingie ring, the jingie ring
Here I gae round the jingie ring
And through my merry-ma-tanzie

Honey is sweet, and so is he,
So is he, so is he
Honey is sweet, and so is he,
About the merry-ma-tanzie

Apples are sour and so is he
  He's married wi a gay gold ring
A gay gold ring's a cankerous thing
  Now they're married, I wish them joy
Father and mother they must obey
  Loving each other like sister and brother
We pray this couple may kiss together
Chambers, 1842

THE WADDS

O it's hame, and it's hame, and it's hame, hame, hame
I think this night I maun gae hame
Ye had better light, and bide aa night
And I'll choose you a bonny ane

O wha will ye choose, an I wi you bide?

The fairest and rarest in aa the countryside
I'll set her up on the bonny pear-tree
It's straught and tall, and sae is she
I wad wauk aa night her love to be

I'll set her up i the bank dike
She'll be rotten ere I be ripe
The corbies her auld banes wadna pike

I'll set her up on the high crab-tree
It's sour and dour, and sae is she
She may gang tae the mools unkissed by me

She's for another, and no for me
I thank you for your courtesie
Chambers, 1842

THE WIND BLOWS HIGH

The wind, the wind, the wind blows high
Snow is fallin from the sky
Tell me, tell me, who she loves
For the one and two and three

She is handsome, she is ugly
She is the one from the golden city
Tell me, tell me, who she loves
For the one and two and three

Gavin Ford says he loves you
  Stamp your feet if you hate him
Clap your hands if you like him.
Glenrothes, 1981

The wind, the wind, the wind blows high
The rain comes pattering from the sky
[Jenny Johnson] says she'll die
For the lad of the rolling eye

She is handsome, she is pretty
She is the flower of the golden city
She's got lovers, one two three
Pray and tell me who they be

[Johnny Gammie] is her lover
Now and then he's waiting for her
Lash the whip and away we go
Up the Castle Races oh
Durris, Aberdeenshire, 1907, GD

There Came Three Jews

There came three Jews from the land of Spain
To call upon my sister Jane
My sister Jane is far too young
I cannot bear her chattering tongue

Go away Corkscrew!

My name is not Corkscrew
I stamp my foot and away I go

Come back, come back, your coat's so green
And choose the fairest one you've seen

The fairest one that I can see
Is bonnie wee Jean, will ye come to me?
No!

Ye dirty wee rat, ye'll no come oot
No come oot, no come oot
Ye dirty wee rat, ye'll no come oot
To help me wi aa ma washing

The same applies to you, sir
E-I-O sir

Now I've got the Prince of Wales
To help me with my washing
Edinburgh, Ritchie, 1965

Two Dukes

Here are two dukes arriving
Arriving, arriving
Here are two dukes arriving
My ramsy tamsy telimsay

What is your good will, sir?

My will, sir, is to get married

Take one of my fair daughters

They are all so black and so browsy
They sit on the sides o Rousay
They have no chains about their necks
And they are all so black and so browsy

Good enough for you, sir

Before I ride the cities so wide
I will take Miss [*name of player*] to be my bride
Aberdeenshire, 1910, GD

Water Wallflower

Water water wallflower
Growing up so high
We are all maidens
And we all must die

Except [Mary Morrison]
The fairest of us all
She can dance
And she can sing
And she can knock us all down

Fie fie fie and shame
Turn your back to the wall again
Glasgow, 1960s / 70s

We Are Three Brethren

We are three brethren come from Spain
All in French garlands
We are come to court your daughter Jean
And adieu to you, my darlings

My daughter Jean she is too young
She cannot bide your flattering tongue

Be she young or be she old
It's for a bride she must be sold

A bride a bride she shall not be
Till she go through this world with me

Come back, come back you courteous knights
Clear up your spurs, and make them bright

Smell my lilies, smell my roses
Which of my maidens do you choose?

Are all your daughters safe and sound?
Are all your daughters safe and sound?

In every pocket a thousand pounds
On every finger a gay gold ring
Chambers, 1842

WEARY WEARY WAITING

Weary weary waiting on you
I shall wait no longer on you
Three times I've whistled on you
Are you coming out?

I'll tell mamma when I get home
The boys won't leave the girls alone
They pull my hair and break my comb
I'll tell mamma when I get home
Edinburgh, Rymour, 1911

When Grandmama Met Grandpapa

When grandmama met grandpapa
They danced the minuet
The minuet was too slow
They danced another step
With a heel toe heel toe
Give it a kick, give it a kick, give it a kick
That's the way to do it
Bake that cake and turn around
That's the way they do it
Hands up, stick-em-up, drop down dead
That's the way they do it
Temple, Glasgow, 1960s/70s

Who'll Come in Tae Ma Wee Ring?

Who'll come in tae ma wee ring, tae ma wee ring, tae ma wee ring
Who'll come in tae ma wee ring, tae make it a wee bit bigger?

I'll come in tae your wee ring, tae your wee ring, tae your wee ring
I'll come in tae your wee ring, and make it a wee bit bigger

Choose, choose, wha ye'll tak, wha ye'll tak, wha ye'll tak
Choose, choose, wha ye'll tak, a lassie or a wee laddie?

I wouldnae hae a lassie-o, a lassie-o, a lassie-o
I wouldnae hae a lassie-o, I'd raether hae a wee laddie

Bee baw babbity, babbity, babbity
Bee baw babbity, a lassie or a wee laddie, laddie, laddie
Castlemilk, Glasgow, late 1980s

WHO'S GOT THE BALL?

Alla balla alla balla
Who's got the ball?
I haven't got it
It isn't in my pocket
Alla balla alla balla
Who's got the ball?
Rottenrow, Glasgow, 1960s/70s

WILL YE LAY THE CUSHION DOON?

Hey, bonny lassie, will ye lay the cushion doon?
Will ye lay the cushion doon?

Wheat straw's dirty, dirties aa yer goon
Hey, bonny lassie, lay the cushion doon
Forfar, 1948

You Are Het

Counting and counting out

We are particularly rich in rhymes for counting, deciding who
is to chase or be chased, or who is to be on which side in a
game. Many of the rhymes celebrate what seems nonsense
language, used to enjoy the sounds and to demonstrate feats
of memory.

1 2 3 4
Mary at the cottage door
Eating cherries off a plate
Doon fell the summer seat
I've a kistie, I've a creel
I've a barrelie fu o meal
To ser' my bairnies till't be done
Come teetle, come tottle, come 2 1
Rymour, 1911

1 2 3, Ma Mammy Caught a flea
She peppered it and salted it and had it for her tea
She didn't like it so she gave it to her son
He didn't like it so he threw it up the lum
Rottenrow, Glasgow, 1960s/70s

1 2 3, My Mither Got a flea
She peppered it, and salted it, and put it in her tea
When she put the sugar in, it floated on the top
And when she put the milk in, it went pop pop
Rymour, 1911

1 potato, 2 potato, 3 potato, 4
5 potato, 6 potato, 7 potato more
Penny in the river
Penny in the sea
Penny in the ocean
And out pops she
Glasgow, 1960s/70s

A B C, my grannie caught a flea
She roasted it, and toasted it and had it for her tea
Glasgow, 1991

As I was in the kitchen
Doing a bit of stitching
Old Baldie Humle
Cam an stole ma thumle
I up wi a wee cherry stone
An struck him on the knuckle-bone
You are out, out goes one and out goes she
Argyllshire, 1901

Black bau, grey clüd
Green grass, tap rüd
Stand du der fur do's oot
Shetland, Saxby, 1932

Black sugar, white sugar, strawberry jam
Tell me the name of your young man
Forfar, 1948

Christopher Columbus was a very old man
And he sailed through the ocean in an old tin can
And the waves grew higher and higher and over
5, 10, 15
Glasgow, 1993

Cowboy Joe fi Mexico
Hands up, stick them up
Drop your guns and pick them up
O-U-T, spells out
Dalkeith, 1997

Eachy peachy hallagolum
Pitchin tatties up the lum
Santa Claus got one in the bum
Eachy peachy hallagolum
Glasgow, 1960s/70s

Eenertee, feenertee, fichertie, feg
Ell, dell, dolman's egg
Irkie, birkie, starry rock
Ann tan two's Jock
Black puddin, white troot
That shows you're oot
Forfar, 1948

Eenie meanie destaneenie
You are the one and only
Education, liberation
I like you
Down down baby, down by the roller-coaster
Slippin, slidin, no place to go
Caught you with your boyfriend, naughty naughty
Didn't do the dishes, lazy lazy
Jump out the window, flippin crazy
Culbokie, Ross-shire, 2006

Eenie meenie acha racha
Ex pert dani nacha
Oot skoot pocks a leen jecks
You are not het
East End, Glasgow, 1997

Eenie meenie, clean peenie
If you want a piece and jelly
Just walk out
Argyllshire, 1901

Eenie meenie macca racca
Eenie meenie macca racca rah ray
A dominaca lollypopa
Don doon doosh out
Glasgow, 1991

Eenie meenie maka naka
El do dona macka
Sugar lolly popa
Rumdum squash
Glasgow, 1991

Eenie meenie macca racca
Day daw dominacca
Chicken poppa, lolly poppa
An O-U-T spells out
Moray, 2006

Eenie meenie macca racca
Om pom pacca racca
Eenie meenie macca racca
Om pom push
Glenrothes, 1981, SSS

Eenie meenie makaraka
Diri diri dominaka
Pom pom push
Chinese ju-ju 1, 2, 3
Alla walla webstick
Out she goes
Temple, Glasgow, 1960s/70s

Eenie meenie miney mo
Sit the baby on the bo
Out pop 1, out pop 2
Out pop another one
And that means you
East End, Glasgow, 1997

Eenie meenie miney mo
Sat the baby on the po
When it's done wipe its bum
Fling the paper up the lum
You are out with a dirty dish clout
Right over your shoulder just like this
Penny on the river, tuppence on the sea
Threepence on the ocean and out pops she
Bellahouston, Glasgow, 1960s/70s

Eenti teenti terry merry, am tam tosh
Look under the bed and catch a wee fat mouse
Cut it up in pieces, fry it in the pan
Mind you leave some gravy for the wee fat man
West Lothian, 1990s

Eentie teentie, tippenny bun
The cat geed oot tae get some fun
She got some fun, she played drum
Eentie teentie, tippenny bun
Hendry & Stephen, 1982

Eenty feenty halligolun
The cat went out to get some fun
He got some fun and tore his skin
As eenty feenty halligolin
Argyllshire, 1901

Eenty, feenty, figgery fell
Ell, dell, dominell
Auntie, Tantie, torry-row
An, Tan, Teesy Jo
You are out
Castlemilk, Glasgow, 1980s

Eeny meany acha racha ex pert dani nacha
Oot skoot pocks a leen jecks
You are not het
East End, Glasgow, 1997

Eerie orrie, eekerie am
Pick me, mick me, shick me sham
Orum scorum, pick-ma-norum
Shee sho sham shutter – you're out
Edinburgh, Rymour, 1919

Eetle ottle black bottle
Eetle ottle out
If you want a piece and jam
Please step out
Dingwall, 1950s

Eeetle ottle black bottle
Eetle ottle out
Shining on the mantelpiece
Like a shining threepenny piece
Eeetle ottle black bottle
Eetle ottle out
Edinburgh, 1951

Ezeenty teenty figgery fell
Ell dell dominell
Arky parky taurry rope
Ann tan toosey joke
Jock went out tae sell his eggs
Who did he meet but bandy legs
Bandy legs and tippy toes
That's the way the ladies go
You are out
Glasgow, 1960s/70s

Gem, gem, ba, ba
Twenty lasses in a raw
No a lad amang them aa
Gem, gem, ba, ba
Rymour, 1919

Ibble obble
Chocolate bubble
Ibble obble out
Pack your case and step right out
Turn a dirty dish cloth inside out
Glasgow, 1991

If you'd have been
Where I have been
The fairy queen
You'd have been out
Out goes one, out goes two
Out goes another one
And that means you
Rottenrow, Glasgow, 1960s/70s

In Liverpool there is a school
And in that school there is a class
And in that class there is a desk
And in that desk there is a book
And in that book there is an
A, B, C, D, E, F, G
Rottenrow, Glasgow, 1960s/70s

Ingle angle, silver bangle
Ingle angle, A, B, C, D,
E, F, G, H, I, J, K, L,
M, N, O, P, Q, R, S, T,
U, V, W, X, Y, Z Zombie
Ingle angle, silver bangle
Glasgow, 1991

Inty, tinty, heathery, blethery, bamfalourie
Hootery, scootery, ding dong, long tong
Salmonella (or 'semolina') fill your pipe
And you are out
West Lothian, 1990s

It hit, catch the nit
You are not it
Glasgow, 1993

I've as many bawbees as I can spend ava
And gin ye need a shillin, man, it's I could
    gie ye twa
Rymour, 1919

Maister Mundy, how's your wife?
Very sick an like to die
Can she eat any meat?
Just as much as I can buy
She makes her porridge very thin
A pound of butter she puts in
Black puddin, white troot
Eerie-orie, you're oot
MacLennan, 1909

Mammy, Daddy, tell me true
Who should I be married to?
Tinker, tailor, soldier, sailor
Rich man, poor man
Beggar man, thief
Rottenrow, Glasgow, 1960s/70s

Me and the minister's wife coost oot
Guess ye what it was aa aboot
Black pudding, dish-cloot
Eerie orie, you are oot
Hendry & Stephen, 1978

One ery two ery
Tackery teeven
Kiloma crackery
Tenory leeven
Wish wash, bang a wish
Little wee sting horse
Easter Ross, 1920s

Oor wee Jeanie had a nice clean peenie
Guess what colour it was
Red
R-E-D spells RED, and O-U-T spells OUT
Glasgow, 1957, SSS

Oozie oozie arns, you're withoot the harns
Up and doon aa the toon, glowerin at the starns
Eeksie peeksie, turn aboot
One two, you are oot
Perthshire, Rymour, 1919

Oranges, oranges, four for a penny
My father was drunk from eating too many
Be bo Baldy Snout
I am in and you are out
Argyllshire, 1901

P-I-G spells PIG
T-I-G spells TIG
You are out
With a dirty washing clout
Right over your left ear
Just like this
Glasgow, Davison, 1960s/70s

Sing a song, a ming, a mong, a carlin and a kit
And them at disna like butter, put in their
    tongue and lick
Mintlaw, Rymour, 1919

Six white horses in a stable
Pick one out and call it Mabel
Maypole butter, maypole tea
M-A-Y-P-O-L-E
John Street, Glasgow, 1960s/70s

Sour-milk Jenny, a pint for a penny
Stop your horse and give me a drink
Sour-milk Jenny, you are out
Kingarth, Bute, Rymour, 1911

There's a donkey in the grass
With a bullet up his ass
Pull it out, pull it out
Be a good Boy Scout
And if you do what colour would the blood be?
Glasgow, 1993

Three white horses in a stable
Pick one out and call it Mabel
If it's Mabel, set the table
Three white horses in a stable
Edinburgh, Lomax, 1951

Two wan picks a man
1, 2, 3, 4, 5, 6, 7, 8, 9, 10
11, 12, 13, 14, 15, 16, 17, 18, 19, 20
Twenty-one picks a man and who should
    that very lucky man be?
Glasgow, 1991

In the Roaring Playground

A few of the longer songs in these sections are performance pieces, used while guising at Halloween, or formerly in urban 'back court concerts', but most were used to aid, support and accompany play, to caw the ropey, to bounce with one or more balls and to perform small dramatic 'dance' routines. They are now chiefly sung for synchronised hand clapping with one or more partners.

KATIE BAIRDIE HAD A ZOO

Animals

As I went o'er the Brig o Dee
I spied a dead horsie
I oned it, I twoed it, I threed it
I foured it, I fived it, I sixed it
I sevened it, I ate it
Aberdeenshire, 1951

Beetle, beetle go away, go away
I'm afraid you cannot stay, cannot stay
Remember what the Brown Owl said
No to beetle in a bed, in a bed
Glasgow, 1960s/70s

Cat's got the measles, dog's got the flu
Chicken's got the chicken pox and so have you
Moray, 2006

Happy birthday to you
You live in the zoo
You look like a monkey
And you smell like one too
Moray, 2006

Happy birthday to you
You were born in the zoo
With the donkeys and the monkeys
And the kangaroos like you
Glasgow, 1960s/70s

Hi gee-up ma cuddie
Ma cuddie is ower the dyke
An if ye touch ma cuddie
Ma cuddie will gie ye a bite
Dingwall, 1950s

Horsey, horsey, don't you stop
Just let your feet go clippety clop
Your tail go swish and your wheels go round
Giddy-up to London Town
Rottenrow, Glasgow, 1960s/70s

Horsey, horsey, living in a stable
Does not know his two times table
The teacher says you're not able
Horsey, horsey, living in a stable
Rottenrow, Glasgow, 1960s / 70s

Hurley burley, tramp the trace
The coo shet owre the market place
East or west? The craw's nest?
Where does this poor man go?
Dunfermline, Rymour, 1919

I had a little chicken
It wouldn't lay an egg
I poured hot water all
Up and down its legs
I giggled, and giggled
And giggled all day
Cause hard-boiled eggs
Were all it would lay
Glasgow, 1960s / 70s

I know a teddy bear
Blue eyes and curly hair
Roly-poly through the town
Knockin all the people down
I know a teddy bear
Glasgow, 1992

I see the gouk
But the gouk sees na me
Atween the berry buss
An the aipple tree
MacLennan, 1909

I'm a bow-legged chicken
I'm a cock-a-doodle-doo
I missed my bus at half past two
I went to the cafe, to have a cup of tea
I ate too many sausages, whoops, pardon me
Addiewell, 1996

Jean Jean Jean
The cat's at the cream
Suppin wi her fore-feet
An glowerin wi her een
MacLennan, 1909

Kate the spinner
Come doon to your dinner
An taste the leg of a frog
All you good people
Look owre the kirk steeple
An see the cat play wi the dog
MacLennan, 1909

King Billy had an orange cat
It sat upon the fender
And every time the Pope passed by
It shouted 'No surrender'
Beads an beads an holy beads
Beads an holy waater
The priest fell doon the chapel stairs
An made an awfu clatter
Greenock, 1950s

Lingle, lingle, lang tang
Our cat's dead
What did she die wi?
Wi a sair head
Aa you that kent her
When she was alive
Come to her burial
Atween four and five
Chambers, 1842

My wee monkey's dead
He's lying in its bed
He cut his throat
With a five pound note
My wee monkey's dead
Glasgow, 1960s/70s

No a beast in aa the glen
Laid an egg like Picken's hen
Some witch-wife we dinna ken
Sent a whitterit frae its den
Sook'd the bluid o Picken's hen
Picken's hen's cauld and deid
Lyin on the midden heid
Dumfriesshire, Rymour 1928

Not last night but the night before
Three wee monkeys came to my door
One with a banjo, one with a drum
One with a pancake stuck to its bum
East End, Glasgow, 1997

Once we had an orange cat
It sat upon the fender
Every time it burnt its tail
It said, 'We'll no surrender'
Cranhill, Glasgow, 1960s/70s

Pussiker, pussiker, myawie, myawie
Far will ye get mait in the snyawie?
I'll gae doon tae the boggies, and worry
    the hoggies
And I'll get beenies to gnyawie, gnyawie
New Deer, SSS

Rin Tin Tin swallowed a pin
He went to the doctor
The doctor wasnae in
He chapped the door
And the nurse came oot
Thumped in the belly
And the pin fell oot
Rottenrow, Glasgow, 1960s/70s

Roon, roon rosie, Cappie, Cappie shell
The dog's away tae Campbeltown tae
    buy a new bell
If ye'll no tak it, I'll tak it mysel
Roon, roon rosie, Cappie, Cappie shell
Argyllshire, 1901

Sanny Coutts' little doggies
Little doggies, little doggies
Sanny Coutts' little doggies
Licket Sanny's mou, man
Sanny ran aboot the stack
An aa's doggies at's back
An ilka doggie gied a bark
An Sanny ran awa, man
Rymour, 1928

The cattie rade to Passelet
To Passelet, to Passelet
The cattie rade to Passelet
Upon a harrow tine, O
'Twas on a weetie Wednesday
Wednesday, Wednesday
'Twas on a weetie Wednesday
I missed it aye sin-syne, O
Chambers, 1842

The lion and the unicorn
Fighting for the crown
Up starts the little dog
And knocked them baith down
Some gat white bread
And some gat brown
But the lion beat the unicorn
Round about the town
Chambers, 1842

The parson had a witty coo
And she was wondrous wise
The coo she danced a hornpipe
And gie the piper a penny
To play the same tune owre again
The corn rigs are bonny
New Pitsligo, SSS

Three wee mice skating on the ice
Singing, 'Polly Wolly Doodle all the day'
The ice was thin and they all fell in
Singing, 'Daddy, mammy, daddy, ah'm away'
Glasgow, 1992

Wee cheetie pussie o, rinnin through
    the hoosie o
The parritch pat fell aff the fire and
    burnt aa its feetie o
Edinburgh, 1909

Wee chuckie birdie, toll lol lol
Laid an egg on the window sole
The window sole began to crack
An wee chuckie birdie roared and grat
Dumfriesshire, Rymour, 1928

A WEE BIRD CAM

A wee bird cam tae ma wee door
I thocht it was a sparra
I lifted up its hairy leg
And spanked its wee terrara
Anniesland, Glasgow, 1960s / 70s

A wee bird cam tae oor ha door
Ah thocht it was a sparra
For it began tae whistle tae
The man they cry O'Hara

Ah threw the bird a thrupenny bit
Ah didny think ah hud yin
The wee bird widny pick it up
Because it wis a dud yin
Glasgow, 1950s

CLASH-PYOTIE

Clash-pyotie, clash-pyotie, sits on the tree
Dings doon aipples, one two three

One to the master, and one to the man
And one to the laddie that ca's the caravan

But nane to the clash-pyot, what will we gie
Gie to the clash-pyot that sits on the tree?
A barrowfu o muck, and a barrowfu o hay
And we'll cairry the clash-pyotie doon to
    the Bay
Mintlaw, Rymour, 1919

CLEAVERIE, CLEAVERIE

Cleaverie, cleaverie, sit i the sun
And let the weary herdies in
Aa weetie, aa wearie
Aa droukit, aa drearie

I haena gotten a bite the day
But a drap o cauld sowens
Sitting i the blind bole

By cam a cripple bird
And trailed its wing owre
I up wi ma rung
And hit it i the lug

Cheep cheep, quo the bird
Clock clock, quo the hen
Fient care I, quo the cock
Come na yon road again
Chambers, 1842

DINGLE, DINGLE DOUSY

Dingle, dingle dousy
The cat's at the well
The dog's awa to Musselburgh
To buy the bairn a bell

Greet, greet, bairnie
An ye'll get a bell
If ye dinna greet faster
I'll keep it to myself
Chambers, 1842

FROGGIE CAME COURTING

Froggie cam to the mill door
Kye my dearie, kye me
Saddled and bridled and shod afore
Kye my dearie, kye me

Kye my dearie, kill a geerie
Kye my dearie, kye me
Wi my rum strum bumereedle
Bullabulla rig dum
Rig dum boomie meerie kye me

When they were all at supper sat
In cam the kittlin and the cat

It's next cam in the sulky deuk
And she plucket Froggie out o the neuk

Wouldna that mak a hale heart sair
To see sic a company gathered wi care

And wadna that mak a hale heart crack
To see sic a company aa gone to wrack
King Edward, GD

There was a moosie in a mill
Kiltie keerie ca ye me
And a froggie in a well
Rigdum bummaleerie ca ye me
Ca ye deemie, ca ye keemie
Ca ye deemie, ca ye me
Streem stram pummareedle, rally-bally rantan
Rigdum bummaleerie ca ye me
Calder Ironworks, Glasgow, Rymour, 1911

I Had a Little Monkey

I had a little monkey, his name was Charlie Sim
I put him in a bathtub to see if he could swim

He drank all the water, he ate all the soap
We had to get the doctor before he could choke

In came the doctor, in came the nurse
In came the lady with the big fat purse

Out went the doctor, out went the nurse
Out went the lady with the big fat purse
Glasgow, 1960s/70s

I Had a Wee Broon Hen

I had a wee broon hen, I liked it very well
An oh aboot ma wee hen a story I will tell

I sent it fur the messages, away oot in the rain
An ma wee broon hen never came back again

I'll hae a funeral for ma wee hen
Ah'll hae a funeral for ladies and gentlemen

Ladies and gentlemen come ben for ma wee hen
For ma wee broon hen, it never came back again
Glasgow, 1960s / 70s

My Doggie and I

My doggie and I gaed doon to the well
My doggie fell in and he drooned himsel
He drooned himsel and naebody saw im
And fat will come o me, my doggie's awa

Ac wow-ow, my doggie's deid
Bowf-bow-ow, my doggie's deid
Sae weel I can spin at a spangi thread
But bowf-bow-ow, my doggie's deid
Aberdeenshire, SSS

MY WEE FARMYARD

I had a wee cock, and I loved it well
I fed my cock on yonder hill
My cock, lily-cock, lily-cock, coo
Every one loves their cock, why should not
    I love my cock too?

I had a wee hen, and I loved it well
I fed my hen on yonder hill
My hen, chuckie, chuckie
My cock, lily-cock, lily-cock, coo
Every one loves their cock, why should not
    I love my cock too?

Other animals are added in turn, until
the last verse is:

I had a wee pig, and I loved it well
I fed my pig on yonder hill
My pig, squeakie, squeakie
My cat, cheetie, cheetie
My dog, bouffie, bouffie
My sheep, maie, maie
My duck, wheetie, wheetie
My hen, chuckie, chuckie
My cock, lily-cock, lily-cock, coo
Every one loves their cock, why should not
    I love my cock too?
Chambers, 1842

Pussy Pussy

Poussie poussie baudrons, where hae ye been?
I've been at London seeing the queen
Poussie poussie baudrons, what got ye there?
I got a guid fat mousikie rinning up a stair
Poussie poussie baudrons, what did ye do wi't?
I put it in my meal-poke to eat it to my bread
Chambers, 1842

Pussy pussy paten, where hae ye been?
I hae been in London seeing the Queen
What got ye there? Sour milk and cream
Where's my share? In the black dog's tail
Where's the black dog? In the wood
Where's the wood? The fire burned it
Where's the fire? The sea drowned it
Where's the sea? The bull drunk it
Where's the bull? The butcher killed it
Where's the butcher?
Ten miles below my granny's door, eating
    two salt herrin and two raw potatoes
Argyllshire, 1901

Robin Lad

Guid-day now, bonnie Robin lad
How lang hae ye been here?
O I've been bird about this glen
For mair three thousand year

Singing father linkum linkum
Singing father linkum dear
O sic a bird as Robin is
Ne'er sat among the brier

I've biggit on yon bonnie bank
This mair three thousand year
And I wad mak my testament
Guid man, if you would hear

Now, in there cam my Lady Wren
Wi mony a sigh and groan
'O, what care I for aa the lads
If my wee lad be gaun?'

Then Robin turned him round and said
E'en like a little king
'Go, pack ye frae my chamber-door
Ye little cuttie quean'
Moffat, 1933

SINNE SINNE SET YE

Sinne sinne set ye
Owre the hill o Benachie
And lat the peer herdie hame
Till's caul meal an bree
The black chicken an the grey
Has suppit amon't aa day
He up wi's club
And gae't o the lug
Peek peek, quo the chicken
Care care, quo the hen
Deil care, quo the cock
Ye sud a come to yer bed fin I bade ye
New Pitsligo, GD

TAM TAITS

'What ca they you?'
'They ca me Tam Taits!'
'What do ye?'
'Feed sheep and gaits!'
'Where feed they?'
'Down i' yon bog!'
'What eat they?'
'Gerse and fog!'
'What gie they?'
'Milk and whey!'
'Wha sups it?'
'Tam Taits and I!'
Chambers, 1842

The Animals Went In

The animals went in one by one
Some were deaf and some were dumb
Ee-i – ee-i – ee-i – o, Eldorado

The animals went in two by two
Some wore clogs and some wore shoes

The animals went in three by three
Some were big and some were wee

The animals went in four by four
Some through the windy and some through the door

The animals went in five by five
Some were dead and some were alive

The animals went in six by six
Some with crutches and some with sticks

The animals went in seven by seven
Some play hell and some play heaven

The animals went in eight by eight
Some were early some were late

The animals went in nine by nine
Some with whisky some with wine

The animals went in ten by ten
If you don't know the story, I'll tell you it again
Glasgow, 1960s/70s

The Craw's Killed the Pussie

The craw's killed the pussie oh
The craw's killed the pussie oh
The muckle cat sat doun and grat
In Willie's wee bit housie oh

The craw's killed the pussie oh
The craw's killed the pussie oh
An aye an aye the kitten cried
'Oh, wha'll bring me a mousie oh?'
Moffat, 1933

There Was a Wee Bit Mousikie

There was a wee bit mousikie
That lived in Gilberaty o
It couldna get a bite o cheese
For cheetie-poussie-cattie o

It said unto the cheesikie
'O fain wad I be at ye o
If it were na for the cruel paws
O cheetie-poussie-cattie o'
Chambers, 1842

The Soo's Ta'en the Measles

O what will we mak o the auld soo's heid?
It'll mak as guid a toaster as ever toasted breid
A toaster, a fryin pan, or ony mortal thing
O the soo's ta'en the measles and she's deid, puir thing

O what will we mak o the auld soo's lug?
It'll mak as guid a dish-clout as ever dichted mug
A dish-clout, a scourin-clout, or ony mortal thing
O the soo's ta'en the measles and she's deid, puir thing

O what will we mak o the auld soo's tail?
It'll mak as good a souple as ever hung a flail
A souple, a walkin-stick, or ony mortal thing
O the soo's ta'en the measles and she's deid, puir thing
Crossmichael, Rymour, 1919

The Tod

'Eh,' quo the tod, 'it's a braw licht nicht
The win's in the west an the mune shines bricht
The win's in the west an the mune shines bricht
An I'll awa tae the toun o

'I was doon amang yon shepherd's scroggs
I'd like tae been worrit by his dogs
But by my sooth I minded his hogs
The nicht I cam tae the toon o'

He's ta'en the grey goose by the green sleeve
'Eh, you auld witch, nae langer shall ye live
Your flesh it is tender, your bones I maun prieve
For that I cam tae the toun o'

Up gat the auld wife oot o her bed
An oot o the window she shot her auld head
'Eh gudeman, the grey goose is dead
An the tod's been in the toun o'
Buchan, 1962

THREE CRAWS

Three craws sat upon a wa
Sat upon a wa, sat upon a wa aw aw aw
Three craws sat upon a wa
On a cold and frosty morning

The first craw was greetin for its maw

The second craw couldny flee at aa

The third craw fell an broke its jaw

The fourth craw wisnae there at aa
Glasgow, 1950s

WEE COCK SPARRA

A wee cock sparra sat in a tree
A wee cock sparra sat in a tree
A wee cock sparra sat in a tree
Chirpin awa as blythe as can be

Along cam a boy wi a bow an an arra
An he shouted, 'Ah'll get ye, ye wee cock sparra'

Ra boy wi ra arra let fly at the sparra
But he hut a wee man who wiz wheelin a barra

Ra man wi ra barra cam ower wi the arra
He says, 'Dae ye tak me fur a wee cock sparra?'

Ra man hit ra boy though he wisnae his farra
An ra boy stood an glowered, he wiz hurt tae ra marra

An aa this time the wee cock sparra
Wiz chirpin awa on the haft o the barra
Glasgow, 1960s

MY BOYFRIEND GAVE ME AN APPLE

Courting and marriage

Cinderella at the ball
Fell in love with Henry Hall
Henry Hall at the table
Fell in love with Betty Grable
Betty Grable is a star
S-T-A-R
Dumfries, 1960

Cinderella dressed in yella
Went to the ball with a handsome fella
Cinderella dressed in blue
Went to a party and lost her shoe
Rottenrow and Bellahouston, Glasgow, 1960s/70s

Cinderella dressed in yella
Went upstairs to kiss a fella
By mistake she kissed a snake
How many kisses did it take?
Dalkeith, 1997

Down in the heart of Texas with a banjo on my knee
I came from the heart of Texas with a banjo on my knee
Oh dear Louise, I hope you'll marry me
I came from the heart of Texas with a banjo on my knee
Oh no, oh yes, it's amanarita
East End, Glasgow, 1997

Fraser, Fraser, do you love me?
Fraser, Fraser, do you care?
Fraser, will you marry me
In my underwear?
Glasgow, 1960s/70s

Hey, you Monkees, singing on TV
Send me Davy till half past three
If you can't spare Davy, Micky will do
If you can't spare Micky, send the other two
Glasgow, 1960s/70s

I come from chinky China
My home's across the sea
I wash my clothes in China
For two and six a week
Oh Mary, Mary, Mary
You ought to be ashamed
To marry, marry, marry
A man without a hame
Rottenrow, Glasgow, 1960s/70s

I ken something that I'll no tell
Aa the lasses o our town are cruppen in a shell
Except the Flower o [Hamilton] and she's cruppen out
And she has a wee bairn, wi a dish-clout
Lanarkshire, 1842

I love my scout
He takes me out
He buys me chips
To grease my lips
He takes me to the
P-I-C-T-U-R-E-S
Glasgow, 1960s/70s

I'll gie ye a preen to stick in your thoom
To cairry a lady to London toon
London toon's a braw braw place
Aa covered ower wi gold and lace
Hotch her up, hotch her doon
Hotch her into London toon
Calder Ironworks, Glasgow, Rymour, 1911

I'll tell my mammy on Rosemary Ann
She's out walking with a fine young man
High heel shoes and a feather in her hat
What would you do with a sister like that
Bellahouston, Glasgow, 1960s/70s

I've found something that I'll no tell
Aa the lads o our town clockin in a shell
Aa but [Willie Johnson] and he's cruppen out
And he will have [Susie Kerr] without ony doubt
Berwickshire, 1842

Jingle bells are ringing, Mother let me out
My sweetheart is waiting, he's going to take me out
He's going to give me apples, he's going to give me pears
He's going to give me a sixpence to kiss him on the stairs
Gorgie, Edinburgh, Rymour, 1911

Mrs Johnstone lives ashore
With a knocker on her door
When a sailor comes ashore
He knocks at Mrs Johnstone's door
Alla balla alla balla bee
Alla balla A B C
Alla balla alla balla bee
Married to a sailor
Fraser, 1975

My boyfriend gave me an apple
My boyfriend gave me a pear
My boyfriend gave me a kiss on the lips
And threw me down the stair
He threw me over London
He threw me over France
He threw me over the USA
And he lost my underpants
East End, Glasgow, 1996

What a leman will ye gie me gin I gie you a bride?
I'll gie ye [A— B—] to sit doon by your side
Wi the riddle and the girdle
And the gowd aboot his middle
Wi the siller shakin frae his heels
To mak the lasses like him
Aberdeenshire, GD

A Big Ship Was Leaving Bombay

A big ship was leaving Bombay today
Back from those Isles of Man, so they say
There stood [Jeanie] with tears in her eyes
Along came the captain with two big black eyes

Saying darling, oh darling be mine
I'll send you a sweet valentine, valentine
He turned round and kissed me
I ducked and he missed me
A big ship was leaving Bombay today
Rottenrow, Glasgow, 1960s/70s

Ah'm Gaun Awa in the Train

Ah'm gaun awa in the train
And you're no comin wi me
Ah've got a lad o my ain
His name is Kiltie Jamie

He wears a tartan kilt
He wears it in the fashion
And every time he turns roond
I canna keep frae laughin
Glasgow, 1950s

Aye, Ye'll Go

Aye, ye'll go, aye, ye'll go
Whether ye want tae or no
Ye'll go and ye'll get it, and never regret it
Ye'll go, aye, ye'll go, aye, ye'll go

Aye, ye'll go, aye, ye'll go
Whether ye want tae or no
Wee dirty nappies and wee greeting weans
Sign in the book and yer life's no the same
Glasgow, 1960s/70s

Braw News

Braw news is come to town
Braw news is carried
Braw news is come to town
[Mary Foster's] married
First she gat the frying pan
Syne she gat the ladle
Syne she gat the young man
Dancing on the table

Here is a lass with a golden ring
Golden ring, golden ring
Here is a lass with a golden ring
So early in the morning
Gentle Johnnie kissed her
Three times blessed her
Sent her a slice o bread and butter
In a silver saucer

Who shall we send it to
Send it to, send it to?
Who shall we send it to?
To [Mrs Ritchie's] daughter

Braw news is come to town
Braw news is carried
Braw news is come to town
[Sandy Dickson's] married

First he gat the kail-pat
Syne he gat the ladle
Syne he gat a dainty wean
And syne he gat a cradle
Chambers, 1842

Broken-Hearted I Wander

Broken-hearted I wander
At the loss of my brother
He's a jolly jolly fellow
At the battle he was slain

He had a silver sixpence
And he broke it in twae
And he gave me the half o't
Before he went away

If I were an angel
I would fly to the skies
And far beyond the mountains
Where my dear brother lies
Gorgie, Edinburgh, Rymour, 1911

DOON AT BARRALAND

It happened doon at Barraland
He asked me for a dance
Ah knew he was a flyman
But ah had tae take ma chance

His shoes were neatly polished
His hair was neatly combed
And when the dance was over
He asked tae see me home

He promised me a satin dress
He promised me a ring
He promised me a cradle
Tae rock ma baby in

Ah never seen the satin dress
Ah never seen the ring
Ah never seen the cradle
Tae rock ma baby in

Oh, listen, aa you herries
Take this advice fae me
Never let a flyman
An inch above yer knee

But when ma wean is older
Ah'll take it by the hand
And teach it aa the jiggin
Up in the Barraland
Rottenrow, Glasgow, 1960s/70s

DOWN IN YONDER MEADOW

Down in yonder meadow where the green grass grows
There [Lucy Locket] bleaches her clothes
She sang, she sang, she sang so sweet
She sang [Willie Piper[across the street

He hugged her, he kissed her, he took her on his knee
And said, 'Dear [Lucy], I hope we will agree
Agree, agree, I hope you will agree
For tomorrow is our wedding day and I must go'

[Lucy] made a dumpling, she made it awfy nice
She cut it up in quarters and gave us all a slice
Saying, 'Taste it, taste it, don't say no
For tomorrow is our wedding day and I must go'

He hugged her, he kissed her, he bought her a gown
A gown, a gown, a guinea gold gown
He bought her a hat with a feather at the back

A pea-brown cherry on a pea-brown hat
She went down to the draper's at the corner of the street
To buy a pair of blankets and a pair of sheets
And half-a-yard of moleskin to mend [Willie's] breeks
Glasgow, 1960s and Dreghorn, 1886

Down in the meadow where the green grass grows
There Jeannie Redpath bleaches her clothes
She sang and she sang and she sang so sweet
She sang her true love across the street

He kissed her, he cuddled her, he put her tae bed
He sent for the doctor before she was dead
In came the doctor and out went the cat
And in came the man wi the sugarelly hat
Leven, 1960, SSS

DOWN TO THE KNEES

Down to the knees in blood, up to the knees in water
My boots are lined with gold, my stockings lined with silver
A red rose on my breast, a gold ring on my finger,
Tarra ding ding ding, tarra ding ding ding dido

Down to the knees in blood, up to the knees in water
My boots are lined with gold, my stockings lined with silver
I for the pots and pans, I for the man that made them

Tarra ding ding ding, tarra ding ding ding dido
Green peas, mutton pies, tell me where my Maggie lies
I'll be there before she dies, green peas, mutton pies

Three pair of blankets and four pair of sheets
One yard of cotton to mend my Johnny's breeks
Green peas, mutton pies, tell me where my Johnny lies
I'll be there before he dies and cuddle in his bosom
Baby in the cradle, playing with the keys
Maggie in the pea park, picking up the peas
Argyllshire, 1901

HARD UP

Hard up, kick the can
[Jane Thomson]'s got a man
If you want to know his name
His name is [Peter Burgess]

Ah widnae get merried if Ah wis you
Ah widnae get merried if Ah wis you
Ah widnae get merried if Ah wis you
Ah'd rather stay wi ma mammy
Rottenrow, Glasgow, 1960s/70s

Hard up, kick the can
[Sadie]'s got a fancy man
If you want to know his name
His name is [Willy Thompson]
Edinburgh, 1999

I ONCE HAD A BOY

I once had a boy, a bonny sailor boy
A boy you could call your own
He ran away and left me, I dinna ken where
But he left me to wander all alone

One day as I walked by the riverside
Somebody caught my eye
It was that boy, that bonny sailor boy
Wi another young girl by his side

He gave me a look of his bonny blue eyes
And a shake of his lily-white hand
But I walked right by and I never cast an eye
For I hate to be jilted by a boy, by a boy
Edinburgh, Lomax, 1951

I'M A LITTLE DUTCH GIRL

I am a pretty little Dutch girl
As pretty as can be be be
And all the boys in cabaret
Go crazy after me me me

My boyfriend's name is Tony
He comes from Californy
He's got ten-inch toes
A two-inch nose
And this is how my story goes

One day as I was walking
I heard my boyfriend talking
To a sweet little girl with a strawberry curl
And this is what he said to her

I L-O-V-E love you
I K-I-S-S kiss you
And we'll go walking in the
D-A-R-K P-A-R-K, dark park
Bellahouston, Glasgow, 1960s/70s

I've a Laddie in America

I've a laddie in America
I've another in Dundee ay ee ay ee
I've another in Australia
And that's the one who's goin tae marry me ay ee ay ee

First he took me tae the dancin
Then he took me tae my tea
Then he ran away and left me
Wi three bonny bairnies on my knee

One was sittin by the fireside
Another was sittin on my knee
Another was sittin by the doorway
Singin, 'Daddie, daddie, please come back tae me'
Glasgow, 1950s

London Castle

As I gaed up by London Castle
Ten o'clock on a summer's night
There ah spied a bonny lassie
Washin her face in the candlelight

She had boots of patent leather
And her stockings lined with silk
Ma dar aye the red red rosie
Halliloo for Jeannie oh

Jeannie I shall wear your ribbons
Jeannie I shall wear them braw
Jeannie I shall wear your ribbons
Till your laddie gangs awa
Leven, 1960, SSS

MY BOYFRIEND'S NAME

My boyfriend's name is Tony
He lives in Macaroni
With a cherry on his nose and three black toes
And this is how my story goes

One day when I was walking
I saw my boyfriend talking
To the prettiest girl in the whole wide world
And this is what he said to her

I am I really love you
I K-I-S-S kiss you
I jump in a lake and saw a snake
I tiddley I tie
Drop dead
Glenrothes, 1981, SSS

My Girl's a Corker

My girl's a corker, she's a New Yorker
I do most anything to keep her in store
She's got a head of hair, just like a grizzly bear
That's where all my money goes
Roompa roompa roompa pa
Roompa pa, roompa pa
Roompa roompa roompa pa
Roompa roompa pa

She's got a pair of eyes, just like two custard pies

She's got a great big nose, just like a farmer's hose
Aberdeen, Lomax, 1951

My Sailor Laddie

I've been east and I've been west
And I've been in Dundee
And the bonniest lad that ever I saw
He ploughs the raging sea
So away with my sailor laddie
Away with him I'll go

I've been east and I've been west
And I've been in Montrose
And the bonniest lad that ever I saw
He wears the tarry clothes

He rows upo' the ocean
And he sails across the sea
And the sailor wi the curly kep
Oh he's the lad for me

He bade me aye cheer up my hert
He bade me ne'er be dull
He bade me aye cheer up my hert
He wid tak me fae the mull
Dundee, Gatherer, 1985

MY WEE CANARY

Oh I've lost my lad and I care-nae
I've lost my lad and I care-nae
I've lost my lad and I care-nae
A ramshy-damshy-doo

Oh we'll get anither canary
We'll get anither canary
We'll get anither canary
A ramshy-damshy-doo
Glasgow, 1960s

I lost my wee canary, canary, canary
I lost my wee canary, a humphy dumphy doo

I'll need tae get another wan, another wan, another wan
I'll need tae get another wan, a humphy dumphy doo

Oh, I met her in the dance hall, dance hall, dance hall
I met her in the dance hall, a humphy dumphy doo

Oh, red cheeks and roses, roses, roses
Red cheeks and roses, a humphy dumphy doo

Oh, this is the one that I choose, I choose, I choose
This is the one that I choose, a humphy dumphy doo
Rottenrow, Glasgow, 1960s/70s

ONE TWO THREE ALEERIE

One two three aleerie
I spied Mrs Peerie
Sittin on her bumaleerie
Eatin chocolate biscuits
Aberdeen, Lomax, 1951

One two three aleerie
I saw Wallace Beery
Sitting on his bumaleerie
Kissing Shirley Temple
Craigmillar, Edinburgh, 1954, SSS

One two three aleerie
Four five six aleerie
Seven eight nine aleerie
Ten aleerie, postman
Glasgow, 1950s

One two three aleerie
My husband's name is Harry
If you think it's necessary
Look it up in the dictionary
Glasgow, 1960s/70s

QUEEN MARY

Queen Mary, Queen Mary, my age is sixteen
My faither's a fermer in yonder green
He's plenty o money to dress me sae braw
But there's nae bonnie laddie will tak me awa

Each morning I rose and I looked in the glass
Says I tae mysel, what a handsome young lass
Put my hands to my sides and I gave a ha, ha
But there's nae bonnie laddie will tak me awa

One morning a drover came in fae Carlisle
I drapped him a curtsey, he gied me a smile
Now my ain drover laddie I loo aboon aa
And there has come a laddie tae tak me awa
Glasgow, 1960s/70s

THE ONE O'CLOCK GUN

One o'clock, the gun went off
I cannot stay no longer
If I do my ma will say
I play with the boys up yonder

My stockings red, my garters blue
My boots all bound with silver
A red red rose upon my breast
And a gold ring on my finger

Heigh ho for Lizzie o
My bonnie Lizzie o
If I had but one to choose
I'd choose my bonnie Lizzie o
Gorgie, Edinburgh, Rymour, 1911

The World Must Be Coming to an End

I married me a wife, oh aye, oh aye
I married me a wife, oh aye, oh aye
I married me a wife and she's the plague o my life
Oh, the world must be coming to an end, oh aye

I sent her for eggs, oh aye, oh aye
I sent her for eggs, oh aye, oh aye
I sent her for eggs and she fell and broke her legs
Oh, the world must be coming to an end, oh aye

I sent her for cheese and she fell and skint her knees

I sent her for butter and she dropped it in the gutter

I sent her for jam and she brought back ham

I sent her for breid and she drapped doon deid

I bought her a coffin and she fell through the bottom

I buried her in durt and she jumped oot her shurt
Edinburgh and Glasgow, 1950s

WHEN AH WAS SINGLE

When ah was single ah used to comb ma hair
Noo ah'm married ah huvny the time tae spare
It's a life, a life, a weary weary life
Yer better tae be single than tae be a married wife

When ah was single I used a powder puff
Noo ah'm married ah canny afford the stuff

One says, 'Mammie, help me intae ma pram'
Anither says, 'Mammie, gie's a piece and jam'

One says, 'Mammie, help me intae ma bed'
Anither says, 'Mammie, scratch ma wudden leg'

Wan shouts, 'Mammie, help me dae ma sums!'
The ither shouts, 'Mammie, help me scratch ma bum!'

Wan shouts, 'Mammie, take me for a walk'
The ither shouts, 'Mammie, help me wi ma sock'

Wan shouts, 'Mammie, sit me on yer knee'
The ither shouts, 'Mammie, let me climb the tree'
Glasgow, 1950s and 1960s/70s

When I Was a Wee Thing

When I was a wee thing
Just like a little elf
Then aa the meat that e'er I gat
I laid upon the shelf

But when I gat a wifie
She wadna bide therein
Till I gat a hurl-barrow braw
To hurl her out and in

She wadna eat nae bacon
She wadna eat nae beef
She wadna eat nae lang-kail
For fyling o her teeth

But she wad eat the bonnie bird
That sits upon the tree
So gang doun the burn, Davie dear
And I shall follow thee
Moffat, 1933

SWING YER GRANNIE AFF THE WA

Families

Auntie Mary had a canary
Up the leg of her drawers
It pulled a string and began to sing
And doon fell Santa Claus
Maryhill, Glasgow, 1950s

Captain Cook was eatin soup
His wife was eatin jelly
Captain Cook fell in the soup
And burnt his rubber belly
Dingwall, 1950s

Diddle diddle dumpling, my son John
Went to bed with his trousers on
One shoe off and the other shoe on
Diddle diddle dumpling, my son John
Dingwall, 1950s

Doh ray me, when ah wiz wee
Ah used tae peel the tatties
Noo ah'm big an ah can jig
An ah can kiss the laddies
My faither built me a nice wee hoose
Tae keep me frae the laddies
But the roof fell in and ah fell oot
An ah fell in wi the laddies
Glasgow, 1960s

Down in Aberdeen
I met my Auntie Jean
She gave me a tanner to buy a banana
Down in Aberdeen
Rottenrow, Glasgow, 1960s/70s

Grannie in the kitchen
Daein some stitchin
In come a bogey
And chases grannie out
Glasgow, 1992

Hullaballa, hullaballa, sitting on his mother's knee
Crying for a wee bawbee to get some sugar-candy
My wee lad's awa to sea, he'll come back
    and marry me
Silver buckles on his knee, my wee lad's a sailor
Argyllshire, 1901

I lost my wife on Setterday nicht
And cudna tell far to find her
Up in the mune, sellin shune
A penny the piece, they're aa dune
I lost my wife on Setterday nicht
And didna ken far to find her
Ahint the pump I garred her jump
Tally ho the grinder
Forfarshire, Rymour, 1911

Ma mammie says tae me
Wid ye like a cup o tea?
Ah says no no ah like cocoa
Down in the glen
She took me by the hand
All the way tae Barrowland
Ah says no no ah like cocoa
Down in the glen
Glasgow, 1986

Me and my grannie and a great lot mair
Kicket up a row gaun hame frae the fair
By cam the watchman and cried 'Wha's there?'
'Me and my grannie and a great lot mair'
Rymour, 1919

My grandma and your grandma
Were sitting by the fire
My grandma said to your grandma
'I'm going to set your flag on fire'
Singin ah oh
Singin ah oh darlin
Ma grandma
Erskine, 1992

My grannie went doon tae the cellar
A leak in the gas for to see
She lit a match so she'd see better
Oh bring back my grannie tae me
Glasgow, 1992

My mother said that I never should
Play with the gypsies in the wood
And she said if I did
She'd break my head with the teapot lid
Rymour, 1911

My mother, your mother live down the street
18, 19, Marble Street
And every night they have a fight and this is what they say
Boys are rotten, made of cotton
Girls are sexy, made of Pepsi
Boys come from Jupiter to get more stupider
Girls come from Mars to get more bras
Itsy bitsy lollipop
Itsy bitsy bee
All the boys love me
Whitdale, 1994

My mum's Chinese
My dad's Japanese
Look what happened to me
My mum's Chinese
My dad's Japanese
Look I skint my knee
Erskine, 1992

My wife and I lived all alone
In a little wooden house
We call our own
She likes whisky, I like rum
And we both like Wrigley's Spearmint gum
Ha ha ha, hee hee hee
We both like the Addams Family
John Street, Glasgow, 1960s/70s

Oh I want to go home, oh I want to go home
I'm nae gonnie stay in the orphanage no more
The place where the matrons are always indoor
Take me over the sea
The matron'll never catch me
Oh my, I think I shall die
If you don't take me home
Haynes, 1973

Old Grannie Cockalie
Come tae bed and cuddle me
I'll gie ye a cup o tea
Tae keep yer belly warrum
Glasgow, 1994

Over the garden wall
I let my baby fall
My mother came out
And gave me a clout
Over the garden wall
Glasgow, 1960s/70s

Roon an roon the house, tryin tae catch a flea
Mix it up wi butter and tak it ti ma tea
Ah didny want it, ah gied it tae ma chum
Ma chum didny want it, so he flung it up the lum
The lum gave a crack, the hoose gave a shak
And doon came ma grannie in her wee cutty sark
Montrose, 1976, SSS

Swing yer maw, swing yer paw, honey, oh honey
Swing yer maw, swing yer paw, honey baby
Swing yer maw, swing yer paw, swing yer grannie off the wa
Honey, oh baby mine
We're going to the barn dance tonight
Livingston, 2002

This house is awfy smelly
Patricia's making jelly
They canny afford a telly
The Addams Family
John Street, Glasgow, 1960s/70s

Tommy rise and kindle the fire
Turn the gas a wee bit higher
Go and tell your aunt Maria
Baby's got the toothache
Rottenrow, Glasgow, 1960s/70s

Wavy wavy, turn the rope over
Mother's at the butcher's buyin fresh meat
Baby's in the cradle, playin wi a radle
One two three and a porridge
Dirleton, Rymour, 1913

A Big Fat Wummin

If you should see a big fat wummin
Standin at the corner bummin
That's ma mammie
If you should see her wearin glasses
Smilin at each one that passes
That's ma mammie
Glasgow, 1986

If you see a big fat wummin
Standin on the corner bummin
That's ma grannie
Grannie, grannie
Ah'd walk a million feet
Just tae meet ma grannie
Glasgow, 1960s

COULTER'S CANDY

Ally, bally, ally bally bee
Sittin' on yer mammie's knee
Greetin' for anither bawbee
Tae buy mair Coulter's Candy

Ally, bally, ally bally bee
When you grow up you'll go to sea
Makin' pennies for your daddy and me
To buy mair Coulter's Candy

Mammie, gimme ma thrifty doon
Here's auld Coulter comin' roon
Wi' a basket on his croon
Selling Coulter's Candy

Little Annie's greetin tae
What can poor wee Mammie dae
But gie them a penny atween them twae
Tae buy mair Coulter's Candy

Poor wee Jeannie's lookin' affa thin
A rickle o' banes covered ower wi' skin
Noo she's gettin a double chin
Wi' sookin' Coulter's Candy

Johnnie Scott was awfu thin
His banes were stickin through his skin
Noo he's got a double chin
Wi' eatin Coulter's Candy

Allie ballie allie ballie bee
Sittin on your mammie's knee
Greetin' for another bawbee
To buy some Coulter's Candy

Here comes Coulter doon the street
A big lum hat upon his heid
He's been roon aboot a the toon
Singin' an sellin' candy
Various sources, 1960s

DOCTOR, DOCTOR

Oh mother, mother what a cold I've got
Drinking tea and coffee hot
Wrap me up in a nice big shawl
And take me to the doctor

Doctor, doctor shall I die?
No, my darling, you shan't die
Take this medicine twice a day
And that will cure your cold away
Edinburgh, Ritchie, 1965

DOES YER MAW DRINK WINE?

Does yer maw drink wine?
Does she dae it aa the time?
Does she get a funny feeling
When her heid goes through the ceiling?
Does yer maw drink wine?

Does yer maw drink beer?
Does she drink it aa the year?

Does yer maw drink gin?
Does she drink it frae a tin?

Does yer maw drink whisky?
Does it have her feeling frisky?
Glasgow, 1960s / 70s

DON'T GO DOWN THE MINE

A miner was leaving his home for the mine
When he heard his little boy cry
He went to his bedside to see what was wrong
'Daddy, oh Daddy, don't go down the mine

Don't go down the mine, Dad
Dreams will always come true
Daddy, oh Daddy, it'll break my heart
If anything happened to you'
Glasgow, 1960s / 70s

GRANNIE WALKER

Grannie Walker had a coo
It was yellow, black and blue,
Aa the neighbours danced it through
Hooch! cried Grannie Walker

Grannie Walker had a coo
It was yellow, black and blue
It went un'erneath the bed
And tum'lt o'er the chanty
Greenock, 1950s

HAP AND ROW

The wife put on the wee pan
To boil the bairn's meatie o
Out fell a cinder
And burnt aa its feetie o

Hap and row, hap and row
Hap and row the feetie o't
I never kent I had a bairn
Until I heard the greetie o't

Sandy's mother she came in
When she heard the greetie o't
She took the mutch frae her head
And rowed about the feetie o't
Chambers, 1842

MOTHER, MOTHER

Mother, mother I am ill
Send for the doctor up the hill

Up the hill is too far
We will have a motorcar

A motorcar is too dear
We will have a pint of beer

A pint of beer is too strong
We will try a treacle scone

A treacle scone is too tough
We will have an ounce of snuff

An ounce of snuff makes you sneeze
We will have a pound of cheese

A pound of cheese makes you sick
Run for the doctor, quick quick quick
Forfar, 1948

I Once Had a Dear Old Mother

I once had a dear old mother
She was all the world to me
And when I was in trouble
She sat me on her knee

One night as I was sleeping
Upon my feather bed
An angel came from heaven
And told me mum was dead

I woke up in the morning
To see if it was true
Yes, mum had gone to heaven
Up in the sky so blue

So children obey your parents
And do as you are told
For when you lose a mother
You lose a heart of gold
Rottenrow, Glasgow, 1960s/70s

I'm a Little Orphan Girl

I'm a little orphan girl
My mother she is dead
My father is a drunkard
And won't buy me my bread

I sit upon the windowsill
To hear the organ play
And think of my dear mother
Who's dead and far away

Ding-dong, my castle bell
Farewell to my mother
Bury me in the old churchyard
Beside my eldest brother

My coffin shall be white
Six little angels by my side
Two to sing and two to pray
And two to carry my soul away
Edinburgh, Lomax, 1951

MA MAW SAYS

Ma maw says ah've tae go
Wi ma daddie's dinner oh
Champit tatties, chewin steak
An a wee bit currant cake

Ah came tae a river and ah couldnae get across
Ah paid five bob for a scabby auld horse
Ah jumped on its back, its bones gave a crack
And ah played ma fiddle till the boat came back

The boat came back, we aa jumped in
The boat capsized and we aa fell in
Singin don't be weary, aye be cheery
Don't be weary cause we're aa gaun hame
Castlemilk, Glasgow, 1980s

Ma Maw's a Millionaire

Ma maw's a millionaire
Blue eyes and curly hair
Walkin doon Buchanan Street
Wi her big banana feet
Ma maw's a millionaire

Sittin among the Eskimos
Playin the game of dominoes
Erskine, 1992

Sittin among the Eskimos
Showin them how tae wash their toes
Glasgow, 1991

Sittin among the Eskimos
Puttin her finger up her nose
Glasgow, 1960s/70s

Stots my faither off the wa
Like a wee cahoutchie ba
Maryhill, Glasgow, 1950s

My Family

My mummy is a baker
Yummy yummy, yummy yummy

My father is a dustman
Pong pongie, pong pongie

My sister is a show off
How'd yeh like it, how'd yeh like it

My brother is a cowboy
Bang bang, you're dead
Fifty bullets in the head
Turn around, touch the ground
Singing ai yi yippee yippee yi
Apple pie
Singing ai yi yippee yippee yi
Apple pie
Singing ai yi yippee yippee
Dancing like a hippy
Singing ai yi yippee yippee yi
Apple pie
Forres, 2006

WEE O'HARA'S BARRA

Ma Auntie Jean frae Greenock came
Alang wi ma Auntie Lizzie

They gave me a penny tae buy some rock
But ah met wi Wee O'Hara
He said 'Gie me a sook o yer rock
And ah'll gie ye a hurl in ma barra'

Oh, the bonny wee barra's mine
It doesny belang tae O'Hara
Cause the fly wee bloke, he stuck tae ma rock
And ah'm gaunny stick tae his barra
Glasgow, 1950s

When I Was Ane

When I was ane I was in my skin
When I was twa I ran awa
When I was three I could climb a tree
When I was four they dang me o'er
When I was five I didna thrive
When I was sax I got my cracks
When I was seven I could count eleven
When I was aught I was laid straught
When I was nine I could write a line
When I was ten I could mend a pen
When I was eleven I gaed to the weaving
When I was twall I was brosy Wull
Chambers, 1842

When I Was in the Garden

When I was in the garden
I found a penny farthin
I took it to my mother
To buy a baby brother

My brother was a sailor
He sailed the seven seas
And all the fish that he could catch
Was one two three a-larry

My brother's name is Harry
If you think it's necessary
Look it up in the dictionary
Rottenrow, Glasgow, 1960s/70s

YE CANNY SHOVE YER GRANNIE

Oh, ye canny shove yer grannie aff a bus
No, ye canny shove yer grannie aff a bus
Ye canny shove yer grannie
Cause she's yer mammy's mammy
Ye canny shove yer grannie aff a bus

Ye can shove yer other grannie aff a bus
Ye can shove yer other grannie aff a bus
Ye can shove yer other grannie
Cause she's jist yer daddy's mammy
Shove yer other grannie aff a bus
Glasgow, 1950s

THE QUEEN AND WHO ELSE?

Other people

A minister in his pulpit
He couldn't say his prayers
He giggled and he gaggled
Till he fell down the stairs
The stairs gave a crack
And he broke his humpie back
And all the congregation
Gave a quack, quack, quack
Rymour, 1911

All over Johnny's head
The bugs are playin leapfrog
1 2 3 and over, 1 2 3 and over
They play so merrily in every little corner
1 2 3 and over, 1 2 3 and out
Rottenrow, Glasgow, 1960s/70s

Annie Bell, she kens hersel, she lives below the steeple
And every time she rings the bell, she wakens all the people
Kingarth, Bute, Rymour, 1911

Before wee Maggie died, she took me by her side
She offered me a pair of ragged drawers
They were baggy at the knees, and fulla fulla fleas
And that was the end of Maggie's drawers
Glasgow, 1960s/70s

Betty, Betty show us your leg
Show us your leg, show us your leg
Betty, Betty show us your leg
An inch above the knee
Rottenrow, Glasgow, 1960s/70s

Charlie Chat he milk'd the cat
And Dorothy made the cheese
And Feathery Breeks sat at the door
And ca-ed awa the flees
Mintlaw, Rymour, 1911

Christopher and Norma up a tree
K-I-S-S-I-N-G
First comes love, then comes marriage
Then comes a baby in a golden carriage
Dalkeith, 1997

Cobbler, cobbler mend my shoe
Have it done by half past two
Stitch it up and stitch it down
Now I owe you half a crown
Bellahouston, Glasgow, 1960s/70s

Coca-Cola went to town
Pepsi-Cola shot him down
Dr Pepper fixed him up
Turned him into 7UP
Lossiemouth, 2006

Country Geordie, Brig o Dee
Sups the brose an leaves the bree
Wilson, 1993

Cripple Dick upon a stick and Sandy on a soo
Ride awa to Gallowa to buy a pund o oo
Rymour, 1911

Dancin wi a moonman
Doon at the Barrowlands
Dancin wi a moonman
Tae McGregor and his band
When the lights are turned doon low
And they play the rock an roll
Oh it's smashin dancin wi a moo-oo-oo-oon man
Glasgow, 1950s

Down in the jungle where nobody knows
There's a big mama washing her clothes
With a rubadub here, and a rubadub there
That's the way she washes her clothes
Tiddly aye tie a bokey
Tiddly aye tie bokey wokey wokey
That's the way she washes her clothes
Glasgow, 1991

Down in Liverpool
The Beatles go to school
Ringo cannae do his sums
But he can do his drums
Rottenrow, Glasgow, 1960s / 70s

Elvis in the morning
Cliff in the evening
Tommy at suppertime
Put them all together
And love them all the time
So rock rock rock everybody
Twist twist twist everybody
Listen to the TV show
Sugar in the morning
John Street, Glasgow, 1960s / 70s

Francie and Josie
Were sailing down the Clyde
Francie said tae Josie
'Will you be my bonnie bride?'
Josie said 'Aye,
I'll love you till I die'
Sailing doon the Clyde wi Francie
John Street, Glasgow, 1960s / 70s

Geordie Kilordie, the laird o the Knap
Suppit his brose and swallowed the cap
He gaed to the byre and swallowed the coo
'Hey,' said Geordie, 'I'll surely do noo'
MacLennan, 1909

Hey Ena Sharples, how about a date
I'll meet you at the Wagon Train at half past eight
I can do the rhumba, and I can do the splits
And I can lift my petticoat up to my hips
Glasgow, 1960s/70s

Hey, hey, we're the Monkees
Ma maw's a chimpanzee
Ma dad's a hairy gorilla
And he works for the BBC
Glasgow, 1960s/70s

House to let, apply within
Lady put out for drinking gin
Drinking gin, it's an awful sin
Mary goes out and Ethel goes in
Forfar, 1974

I'm only a poor little Ewing
JR's always picking on me
Sue Ellen's a drunk
And Lucy's a punk
And Bobby came out of the sea
Glasgow, 1960s/70s

I'm Shirley Temple, and I've got curly hair
Two big dimples, I wear my skirts to there
And I'm not able to do the Betty Grable
Cause I'm Shirley Temple, and I've got curly hair
I've got hairy legs like Tarzan
I've got the figure like Marilyn Monroe
I've got the hair like Ginger Rogers
And a face like an elephant's toe
Glasgow, 1960s / 70s

Jean, Jean from Aberdeen
Stole a penny from the Queen
The Queen was mad and Jean was glad
Jean, Jean from Aberdeen
Rottenrow, Glasgow, 1960s / 70s

Jean McColl was pinching coal
Pinching coal, pinching coal
Jean McColl was pinching coal
When the wagon caught her bending
Bellahouston, Glasgow, 1960s / 70s

Jean Preen pickit oot the cat's e'en
Wi a needle and a preen
Gaein ower the double-dykes
Playin on the wind-pipes
Forfar, 1948

Jimmy Pimmy, paper hat
Rade a mile upon a cat
When the cat begood to fling
'Hey,' says Jimmy, 'haud her in'
MacLennan, 1909

Jingle bells, Batman smells
Robin flew away
Kojak lost his lollipop
And bought a Milky Way
Glasgow, 1960s/70s

Jingle bells, Batman smells
Robin laid an egg
The batmobile lost a wheel
And the Joker went to bed
Erskine, 1992

(Oh) K-K-K-Katie she swallowed a ha'penny
And twopence worth of chips the night before
The night before that she swallowed a doormat
And now she's swallowed the key of the kitchen door
Temple, Glasgow, 1960s/70s

Katherine Nicolson is a fool
Send her to the ragged school
When she's dead, bile her head
Make it into gingerbread
Edinburgh, 1954, SSS

Lady Queen Ann, she sits in her stand
And a pair of green gloves upon her hand
As white as a lily, as fair as a swan
The fairest lady in aa the land
Chambers, 1842

Leerie leerie, licht the lamps
Lang legs and crookit shanks
Tak a stick and brak his back
And send him to the market
Rymour, 1911

Ma wee lad's a sodger, he lives in Maryhill
Goes to the pub on a Saturday night and buys a half a gill
Goes to the kirk on Sunday, half an hour late
Pulls the buttons off his shirt and puts them in the plate
Glasgow, 1950s

Mademoiselle she went to town, parlez-vous
To buy herself a wedding gown, same to you
All the people in the town
Thought it was a lovely gown
Inky-pinky parlez-vous, same to you
Rottenrow, Glasgow, 1960s/70s

Mary Queen of Scots got her head chopped off
Her head chopped off, her head chopped off
Mary Queen of Scots got her head chopped off
On the 14th of November
Campbeltown, 1956, SSS

Matthew, Mark, Luke, John
Haud the horse till I loup on
Haud it fast, and haud it sure
Till I get owre the misty muir
Chambers, 1842

Matthew, Mark, Luke and John
Hold the horse till I get on
When I got on, I couldna ride
I fell off and broke my side
Argyllshire, 1901

Me me Chinaman
Me feel ill
Me go to doctor
Me get pill
Me go home again
Me go to bed
Me never ever
Have sore head
Rottenrow, Glasgow, 1960s/70s

Mrs McGuire peed in the fire
The fire was too hot, she peed in the pot
The pot was too wide, she peed in the Clyde
And all the wee fishes went up her backside
Glasgow, 1992

Mrs McGuire peed in the fire
The fire was too hot so she peed in the pot
The pot was too round so she peed on the ground
The ground was too flat so she peed on the cat
And the cat ran away with a pee on its back
East Kilbride, 1960s/70s

Mrs Maclean had a wee wean
She didny know how tae nurse it
She gied it tae me, ah gied it some tea
And its bonny wee belly burstit
Glasgow, 1957, SSS

Mrs Mason bought a rubber doll
She washed it, she dried it
And then she let it fall
She sent for the doctor
The doctor couldn't come
Because he had a pimple
On his wee bare bum
Rottenrow, Glasgow, 1960s / 70s

Mrs Murray was in a hurry
To catch the electric train
She fell in the grass
And skinned her
Ask no questions, tell no lies
Shut your mouth and you'll catch no flies
Pollokshields, Glasgow, 1960s / 70s

Mrs Red went to bed
In the morning, she was dead
The policeman came and took her name
And told her never to die again
Bellahouston, Glasgow, 1960s / 70s

Mrs White got a fright
In the middle of the night
Saw a ghost eating toast
Halfway up the lamppost
Rottenrow, Glasgow, 1960s / 70s

Oh the sun shines bright on Charlie Chaplin
His boots are crackin for the want of blackin
And his wee baggy trousers they need mendin
Before they send him to the Dardanelles
Rottenrow, Glasgow, 1960s / 70s

Old Mrs Reilly at the pawnshop door
Baby in her arms an a bundle on the floor
She asked for ten bob, she only got four
An nearly pullt the hinges aff the pawnshop door
Glasgow, 1960, SSS

One, two: Freddie's coming for you
Three, four: You'd better lock the door
Five, six: Get a crucifix
Seven, eight: You'd better stay up late
Nine, ten: Never sleep again
Bellahouston, Glasgow, 1960s/70s

Paddy on the railway, pickin up stones
Along came an engine and broke Paddy's bones
'Well,' said Paddy, 'That's no fair'
'Well,' said the engine man, 'You shouldny uv been there'
Glenrothes, 1981, SSS

Peter Pan drove a van
Over Wendy, now she's bendy
East Calder, 2007

Queen, Queen Caroline
Dipped her hair in turpentine
Turpentine made it shine
Queen, Queen Caroline
Edinburgh, Ritchie, 1965

Rab Haa, the Glasgow glutton
Ate his shirt and left a button
Rab Haa, the Glasgow glutton
Ate the steak and all the mutton
Erskine, 1992

Rabbie Burns was born in Ayr
Now he's doon in George's Square
If you want to see him there
Hop on the bus and dodge the fare
Aberdeen, Lomax, 1951

Romeo the darkie-o
Sells ice-cream-io
If you want a pokie-o
Go to Mr Romeo
Rottenrow, Glasgow, 1960s/70s

Santa Claus came doon the lum
Wi toys for oor wee Minnie
He stole ma mammy's best fur coat
And noo he's in Barlinnie
Balornock School, Glasgow, 1960s/70s

Skinny Malinky Longlegs
Big banana feet
Went tae the pictures
But couldnae find a seat
When the picture started
Skinny Malinky farted
Skinny Malinky Longlegs
Big banana feet
Rottenrow, Glasgow, 1960s/70s

Tam Tam, the midgie man
Lives in a midgie motor
Running along the dyke
And skelpt his head a stoter
Glasgow, 1993

There was a wee man from Govan
He locked himself in the oven
The silly wee ass, he turned on the gas
There was a wee man from Govan
Pollokshields, Glasgow, 1960s/70s

There's a big fat woman
Twice the size of me
She's got hairs on her arms
Like the branches of a tree
She can sing and she can dance
And dae the Heiland Fling
The only thing she cannae dae
Is slim, slim, slim
Glasgow, 1960s/70s

This is the nicht o Halloween, aa the witches to be seen
Some o them black, and some o them green,
    some o them like a Turkey bean
Edinburgh, Rymour, 1911

Tibbie Fowler in the glen
Stealt her mither's black hen
Be she black, or be she fite
Tibbie Fowler got the wyte
Be she rossen, be she raw
Tibbie Fowler ate her aa
New Pitsligo, SSS

Tom Thumb in a cellar
I-Spy Cinderella
Cinderella in a wood
I-Spy Robin Hood
Robin Hood up a tree
I-Spy the bumble-bee
Bumble-bee in a basin
I-spy Perry Mason
Perry Mason is a star
S-T-A-R
Rottenrow, Glasgow, 1960s/70s

Tommy Morgan played the organ
And his father played the drum
And his sister had a blister
In the middle of her bum
Rottenrow, Glasgow, 1960s/70s

Wee chinky chinky man
Tried to milk a cow
Wee chinky chinky man
Didny know how
East End, Glasgow, 1997

Wee Sam a piece and jam
Went to London in a pram
The pram broke and that's the joke
Wee Sam a piece and jam
Glasgow, 1960s/70s

Wee Sam, a piece an jam
Wee Betty, tin a spaghetti
Wee Linda, bottle o ginger
Glasgow, 1993

Wee Tammy Tyrie fell in the feirie
The feire wiz hot, he jamp ee pot
The pot wiz metal, he jamp ee kettle
The kettle wiz bress, he jamp ee press
The press wiz high, he jamp ee sky
The sky wiz blue, he jamp ee soo
The soo gae a roar, he jamp in the boar
The boar gae a loup
And wee Tammy Tyrie landit on eez doup
Forfar, 1948

Wee Willie Winkie, up an doon the toon
Tried to steal a croon, an then turned broon
East Calder, 2007

What's your name? Baldy Bane
What's your other? Ask my mother
Where do you sleep? Among the sheep
Where do you lie? Among the kye
Where do you take your brose?
Up and down the cuddy's nose
Argyllshire, 1901

Where was Johnny when the lights went out?
Up Sauchiehall Street smokin a dowt
The dowt was wee an so was he
Where was Johnny when the lights went out?
Glasgow, 1986

Who went round the house at night?
None but Bloody Tom
Who stole all my chickens away
All but this poor one?
Calder Ironworks, Glasgow, Rymour, 1850s

Aiken Drum

There cam a man to our town, to our town, to our town
There cam a man to our town and his name was Willy Wood
And he played upon a razor, a razor, a razor
And he played upon a razor, and his name was Willy Wood

And his hat was made o the guid roast beef [etc.]
And his coat was made o the haggis bag [etc.]
And his buttons were made o the baubee baps [etc.]

But another man cam to the town,
     and they ca'd him Aiken Drum
And he ate up aa the guid roast beef [etc.]
Chambers, 1842

Archibald

Archibald bald bald
King of the Jews Jews Jews
Bought his wife wife wife
A pair of shoes shoes shoes

When the shoes shoes shoes
Began to wear wear wear
Archibald bald bald
Began to swear swear swear

When the swear swear swear
Began to stop stop stop
Archibald bald bald
Bought a shop shop shop

When the shop shop shop
Began to sell sell sell
Archibald bald bald
He bought a bell bell bell

When the bell bell bell
Began to ring ring ring
Archibald bald bald
Began to sing sing sing

Doh, ray, me, fah, soh, lah, te, doh
Rottenrow, Glasgow, 1960s/70s

BATMAN AND ROBIN

Batman and Robin came to visit me
Took me tae the cafe tae buy a cup a tea
The tea was so delicious ah had another cup
An poor Cinderella had tae dae the washing up
Glasgow, 1993

Batman and Robin
Were lying in bed
Batman moved over
And Robin was dead
Rottenrow, Glasgow, 1960s/70s

COCKABENDY

Cockabendy's lyin sick
Guess ye what'll mend him?
Twenty kisses in a cloot
Lassie, will ye send him?

Hi cock, hi cock
Hi Cockabendy
Crack a loose on Jeannie's wame
For a gill o brandy

Dinna gie the lasses drink
Dinna gie them brandy
Gie them sticks o cinnamon
And lumps o sugar candy

Cockabendy had a wife
He didna ken fou to guide her
He put her on a donkey's back
And then sat on beside her

Cockabendy had a wife
Oh but she was a dandy
She gaed in below the bed
And coupit owre the chanty
Aberdeenshire, GD

Cocky-Bendy's lyin sick
Guess ye what'll mend 'im?
Stap a gully doon 'is throat
That'll sune end 'im

Half a pound o green tea
Half an ounce o pepper
Tak ye that my bonnie lad
And ye'll sune be better
Rymour, 1911

Coco Bendy had a wife
She was awfu dandy
She fell in beneath the bed
An tumbled o'er the chanty
Bellahouston, Glasgow, 1960s/70s

CASEY THE COWBOY

Casey the Cowboy all dressed in red
Went to the graveyard, there lost his head
There was blood on the saddle, blood on the ground
Great big blobs of blood all around

Casey the Cowboy all dressed in blue
Went to the graveyard, there lost his shoe
Casey the Cowboy all dressed in white
Went to the graveyard, there lost his sight
Dingwall, 1976

DAVIE CROCKETT

Born in a tenement at Partick Cross
Had a razor gang of which he was the boss
Carried a razor ten feet wide
With it he slashed all the cops
And threw them in the Clyde
Davie, Davie Crewcut
King of the razor gang
Glasgow, 1950s

Born on a dustbin in Park Square
Davie Crockett did not care
He swept the lums for half a crown
The best chimney sweep in Campbeltown
Davie, Davie Crockett
King of the chimney sweeps
Campbeltown, 1956, SSS

DOWN IN ABERDEEN

Down in Aberdeen
There lives a fairy queen
Her name is Aggie, she's awfy raggy
Down in Aberdeen

Her name is Mary, she's got a canary

Her name is Alice, she lives in a palace
Glasgow, 1960s/70s

GYPSY GYPSY

Gypsy gypsy Caroline
Washed her hair in turpentine
Turpentine will make it shine
Gypsy gypsy Caroline

Gypsy gypsy Caroline
Washed her hair in VP wine
VP wine will make it shine
Gypsy gypsy Caroline

Gypsy gypsy living in a tent
Had no money to pay the rent
The rent man came and threw her out
And now she's living in the roundabout
Rottenrow, Glasgow, 1960s/70s

JOHNNIE JOHNSTON

Johnnie Johnston's ta'en a notion
For to go and sail the sea
He has left his own true lover
Weeping by the willow tree

I will buy you beads and earrings
I will buy you diamonds free
I will buy you silks and satins
Bonnie lassie, marry me

What care I for beads and earrings
What care I for diamonds free
What care I for silks and satins
When my love's forsaken me?
Rymour, 1911

KATIE BAIRDIE

Katie Beardie had a coo
Black and white about the mou
Wasna that a dentie coo?
Dance, Katie Beardie

Katie Beardie had a hen
Cackled but and cackled ben
Wasna that a dentie hen?
Dance, Katie Beardie

Katie Beardie had a cock
That could spin backin rock
Wasna that a dentie cock?
Dance, Katie Beardie

Katie Beardie had a grice
It could skate upon the ice
Wasna that a dentie grice?
Dance, Katie Beardie
Chambers, 1842

Katie Beardie had a cat
That could eat baith moose and rat
Wasna that a daintie cat?
Dance, Katie Beardie
Rymour, 1911

Dolly Bairdie hid a wife
She could use baith fork an knife
Wisna she a dainty wife?
Dance, Dolly Bairdie
Aberdeenshire, SSS

Katie Bairdie hid a wean
Wadna play when it cam on rain
Wasna that a dentie wean?
Dance, Katie Bairdie

Katie Bairdie hid a coo
It was yellow, black and blue
Aa the monkeys i the Zoo
Lauched at Katie Bairdie's coo
Fraser, 1975

Kitty Birdie had a canoe
It was yellow, black and blue
Open your legs and let it through
Dance, Kitty Birdie
Scotland Street, Glasgow, 1991

Jeannie Bairdie had a wean
Somebudy hit it wi a stane
The doactur said it wuz a shame
Dance, Jeannie Bairdie
Paisley, 1961

Katie Bairdie had a soo
It was reid, and black, and blue
Ye needna gang wi peelins noo
For Katie Bairdie's killed her soo
Rymour, 1919

Mary had a little lamb
She put it in the bunker
A wee bit coal got in its eye
And made it do the rhumba
Oompah cha cha cha
Rottenrow, Glasgow, 1960s/70s

Mary had a little lamb
She sat it on the bunker
Pretty Polly came along
And made it do the rhumba
North, south, east, west
I can do the rhumba best
I can do the rhumba best
Dumfries, 1960

Mary had a little lamb
It climbed right up a pylon
Fifty volts went up its jolts
And turned wool into nylon
Dalkeith, 1997

MISS POLLY'S DOLLY

Miss Polly had a dolly who was sick sick sick
And she called for the doctor to come quick quick quick

The doctor came with his bag and his hat
And he knocked at the door with a rat tat tat

He looked at the dolly and he shook his head
And he said, 'Miss Polly, put her straight to bed'

He wrote out a letter for a pill pill pill
'I'll be back in the morning with a bill bill bill'
Glasgow, 1986

NOW THE WAR IS OVER

Now the war is over, Mussolini's dead
He wants to go to Heaven with a crown upon his head
The Lord says, 'No, he's got to stay below
All dressed up and nowhere to go'
Aberdeen, 1951

Now the war is over, Vasoline is dead
He wants to go to heaven with a crown upon his head
But the Pope says, 'No, you'll have to stay below
There's only room for Elvis and his wee banjo'
Glasgow, 1992

As sure as I am leevin the Kaiser's deed
He thocht to gang to heeven with the crown upon his heed
But the Lord said, 'No, stap him doon below
An pour doon his thrapple a pint o molten leed'
Rymour, 1918

OLD KING COUL

Old King Coul was a jolly old soul
And a jolly old soul was he
Old King Coul he had a brown bowl
And they brought him in fiddlers three
And every fiddler was a very good fiddler
And a very good fiddler was he
Fidell-didell, fidell-didell went the fiddlers
And there's no a lass in Scotland
Compared to our sweet Marjorie

Old King Coul was a jolly old soul
And a jolly old soul was he
Old King Coul he had a brown bowl
And they brought him in drummers three
Rub-a-dub, rub-a-dub went the drummers

Twarra-rang, twarra-rang went the trumpeters
Twingle-twangle, twingle-twangle went the harpers
Ha-didell, howdidell went the pipers
Fidell-didell, fidell-didell went the fiddlers
And there's no a lass in Scotland
Compared to our sweet Marjorie
Herd, 1776

ROB TAMSON

Rob Tamson was a sporty lad
He bet a man a fiver
That he could loup Jamaica Bridge
Like Rabbie Burns the diver

The folk that stood aboot the bridge
Kicked up an awfu shindy
For he fell doon the funnel
O the Clutha Number Twenty
Glasgow, 1962

SAKY SAKY PIRN-TAES

Saky Saky Pirn-taes
The snaw's fa'en doun
And ilka lass wi kilted claes
Is rinnin thro the toun

Past the Cross and past the Kirk
And doun the Netherbow
Saky Saky Pirn-taes
I'm waitin on my jo
Moffat, 1933

SALOME

Oh Salome, Salome
You should see Salome
Hands up there, skirts in the air
You should see Salome

Wing it, swing it
You should see her swing it
Hands up there, skirts in the air
You should see her swing it

Her boyfriend, her boyfriend
You should see her boyfriend
Bowler hat, nose in the air
You should see her boyfriend
Glasgow, 1960s/70s

SANDY LIKES

Sandy likes in tansie o
But my delight's in brandy o
Sandy likes in a red red nose
Caller on my Cuddie o

Hey ho for Cuddie o
My bonny bonny Cuddie o
All the world that I wad gie
If I had my Cuddie o
Argyllshire, 1901

SANDY WAUGH

I hae a wee bit Hieland man
His name is Sandy Waugh
He sits upon a puddock-stool
And fine he sups his broth

Sing hey, my bonnie Hieland man
My Sandy trig and braw
Come prinkum prankum, dance wi me
A cock-a-leerie-law

There's herring in the silver Forth
And salmon in the Tay
There's puffins on the auld Bass
And there's bairns that greet aa day
Moffat, 1933

SOME SAY THE DEIL'S DEID

Some say the deil's deid
The deil's deid, the deil's deid
Some say the deil's deid
And buried in Kirkcaldy

Some say he'll rise again
Rise again, rise again
Some say he'll rise again
An dance the Hielan Laddie
Cheviot, 1896

Tarzan

Tarzan in the jungle
Looking for Jane
Jane's in the toilet
Kissing John Wayne

Tarzan in the jungle
Picking up grass
Along came an elephant
And kicked him up the

Tarzan in the jungle
Picking up sticks
Along came an elephant
And pulled doon his knicks

Tarzan in the jungle
Picking up stones
Along came an elephant
And broke all his bones

Tarzan in the jungle
Waiting for a train
Along came an elephant
And called him Baldy Bain
Glasgow, 1960s / 70s

THREE LITTLE ANGELS

Three little angels all dressed in white
Tried to get to heaven on the end of a kite
But the kite end was broken, down they all fell
They couldn't get to heaven so they all went to

Two little angels, all dressed in white

One little angel, all dressed in white

Three little devils all dressed in red
Tried to get to heaven on the end of a bed
But the bed end was broken, down they all fell
They couldn't get to heaven so they all went to

Two little devils all dressed in red

One little devil all dressed in red

Don't be mistaken, don't be misled
They couldn't get to heaven so they all went to bed
Erskine, 1992

THREE MEN THEY WENT A-HUNTIN

Three men they went a-huntin
Tae see what they could find
They came across a mountain
Something left behind
The Englishman said 'mountain'
The Scotsman he said 'nay'
Said Paddy, 'It's a dumplin
The currants have blown away'
Ay tiddly ay ty
Ay tiddle eh
Said Paddy, 'It's a dumplin
The currants have blown away'

Three men they went a-huntin
Tae see what they could find
They came across a lamppost
Something left behind
The Englishman said 'lamppost'
The Scotsman he said 'nay'
Said Paddy, 'It's a policeman
His buttons have blown away'

Three men they went a-huntin
Tae see what they could find
They came across a monkey
Something left behind
The Englishman said 'monkey'
The Scotsman he said 'nay'
Said Paddy, 'It's yer auld man
Badly needin a shave'
Glasgow, 1960

WEE JOHNNIE'S JAURIE

Wee Johnnie's lost his jaurie
Wee Johnnie's lost his jaurie
Wee Johnnie's lost his jaurie
Doon by the Broomielaw

He drapped it doon a stank

He went and got a clothespole

He shoved it doon the stank

But he couldnae reach it

He went and got gunpowder

He rammed it doon the stank

He blew up half of Glasgow

But still he didnae get it

It was in his bloody pocket
It was in his bloody pocket
It was in his bloody pocket
It wisny lost at aa
Glasgow, 1950s

WILLIAM TELL

Come away, come away with William Tell
Come away to the land he loved so well
What a day, what a day when the apple fell
For Tell and Switzerland

Come away, come away with William Tell
To the land, to the land where his trousers fell
Pull them up, pull them up, what an awful smell
For Tell and Switzerland
Rottenrow, Glasgow, 1960s/70s

AWAY UP IN HOLLAND

Travel

Away up in Holland, the land of the Dutch
There is a wee lassie I love very much
Her name is Suzanna, but where is she now?
She's up in the Highlands, milking the cows
Glasgow, 1993

Away up in Scotland, the land of the Scots
There lives a wee lassie who makes porridge oats
She makes them for breakfast, for dinner and tea
She makes them for mammy and daddy and me
Rottenrow, Glasgow, 1960s/70s

Bluebells, duma-duma shells
Eavy, ivy, over
Charlie Chaplin went to France
To teach the ladies how to dance
First the heel and then the toe
Then you do big birlie o
Big birlie o
Edinburgh, Lomax, 1951

Chicka Tony went to London
Just to ride a pony
He stuck a feather in its cap
And called it macaroni
Aberdeen, Lomax, 1951

Chinese government
Chinese government
Black man's daughter
Tra la la la la la la
The wind blows high
From the sky
And out comes [Jeannie]
    with the big black eye
Edinburgh, Lomax, 1951

Chinese men are very funny
Chinese men are very funny
This is the way they count their money
Oocha oocha, Chinese booska
Glasgow, 1990s

Down in Germany
This is what they say
Eesha asha, you're a wee smasher
Saturday, Sunday, school on Monday
Down in Germany – Ole
Rottenrow, Glasgow, 1960s / 70s

Mademoiselle she went to the well
To wash her hands to dry them
To comb her hair, to say her prayers
To catch a ball in the basket
Bellahouston, Glasgow, 1960s / 70s

Scotland England Ireland Wales
All went out to fish for whales
Some got heads and some got tails
Scotland England Ireland Wales
Forfar, 1948

Up and down, up and down
All the way to London town
Swish-swosh, swish-swosh
All the way to King's Cross
Leg swing, leg swing
All the way to Berlin
Heel toe, heel toe
All the way to Jericho
Edinburgh, Lomax, 1951

TEXAS COWBOY JOE

I'm a Texas, Texas Cowboy Joe
And I come from the land that everyone knows
I can ride, I can shoot, I can do the hula-hoop
When the Indians come to town

There's a guy over there, he winks one eye
He says he loves me, but he's telling a lie
His hair don't curl, and his boots don't shine
He ain't got the money, so he won't be mine

All the girls wear red, white and blue
All the boys say 'I love you'
With a wiggle and a wriggle
When the Indians come to town
In the land of Texas
Dalkeith, 1997

I'm a Texas Texas Texas Girl
I live over there not far away
I can jump, I can shoot, I can do the hula-hoop
Cowboys comin to town, yee ha

There's a boy over there who's lost one eye
He says he loves me but he's tellin a lie
He's got curly hair and his boots don't shine
Cowboys comin to town, yee ha

I'm a Texas Texas Texas Girl
My mama left me when I was three
She walks like a wiggle and a wiggle and a woo
So let's do the Texas wig-wam
Dalkeith, 1997

Wha Saw the Forty-Second

Wha saw the Forty-Second
Wha saw them gang awa?
Wha saw the Forty-Second
Marchin doon the Broomielaw?

Some o them had tartan troosers
Some o them had nane ava
Some o them had green umbrellas
Marchin doon the Broomielaw

Some o them had boots and stockins
Some o them had nane ava
Some o them had tartan plaidies
Marchin doon the Broomielaw
Glasgow, 1950s

Wha saw the tattie howkers?
Wha saw them gaun awa?
Wha saw the tattie howkers
Marchin doon the Broomielaw?

Some o them had boots and stockins
Some o them had nane at aa
Some o them had a wee drop whisky
For tae keep the cauld awa
Dingwall, 1950s

I WENT TO A
CHINESE RESTAURANT

Fun and stories

A pin to see a pappy show
A pin to see a die
A pin to see a wee man
Running up the sky
Argyllshire, 1901

A wee cream cookie
For me and the bookie
I wouldnae gie ye a penny for
A wee cream cookie
Rottenrow, Glasgow, 1960s/70s

Abblesy bibblesy
Kebblesy dibblesy
Ebblesy fibbleysey
Wy sedan
Saltcoats, 1950s
The 'Fast Alphabet'

An angel said to me
'Would you like a cup of tea?'
I said, 'No, no, I like cocoa
Better than tea'
Aberdeen, 1951

Are you going to golf, sir?
No, sir
Why, sir?
Because I've got a cold, sir
Where did you get the cold, sir?
Up at the North Pole, sir
What were you doing there, sir?
Catching polar bears, sir
How many did you catch, sir?
One, sir, two, sir
Three, sir, four, sir
Five, sir, six, sir
Seven, sir, eight, sir
Nine, sir, ten, sir
Craigmillar, Edinburgh, 1954, SSS

As I gaed up the apple tree
Aa the apples fell on me
Bake a puddin, bake a pie
Send it up to John MacKay
John MacKay is no in
Send it up to the man in the mune
The man in the mune is mendin his shune
Three bawbees and a farden in
MacLennan, 1909

As I went up a stair
I met a bobby there
Wi his whiskers tied tae the railing
He asked me ma name
I said leave me alane
My name's Treacle Toffee in the Hielands
Bellahouston, Glasgow, 1960s/70s

We're off to the camp in the country, hooray hooray
We're off to the camp in the country, hooray hooray
Apple jam for supper, ham and eggs for tea
Roly poly doon yer belly, hip hip hip hooray
Glasgow, 1950s

Come up and see ma garret
Come up and see it noo
Come up and see ma garret
For it's aa furnished new
A broken cup-an-saucer
A chair wi'oot a leg
A humphy-backit dresser
And a bandy-leggit bed
Glasgow, 1960s/70s

Don't be a fool, stick to the rule
Listen to the message and just act cool
It ain't no joke, so don't sniff coke
Don't drink alcohol and please don't smoke
Glasgow, 1960s/70s

Call-a-cob, maraline
Cast a barrel in a string
Aa them at winna come to this call-a-cob
Shall be weel call-a-cobbled owre again
Wi the rug and the tug and the gray grace horn
Here a tug, there, amang the laird's corn
Whistle and I'll let gae
Rymour, 1911

Far are ye gaein? Across the gutter
Fat for? A pund o butter
Far's yer money? In my pocket
Far's yer pocket? Clean forgot it
Forfar, 1948

Green, white and blue
The cat's got the flu
The dog's got the chickenpox
And so have you
Rottenrow, Glasgow, 1960s/70s

I wanna go home, I wanna go home
To ma ain wee hoose in Barlinnie
You don't need this, you don't need that
You only need a hammer and a chisel
When you get there, they cut off your hair
They put it in a tin-tin-tinnie
And gie it tae the weans in the dinnie
Govan, Glasgow, 1960s/70s

Ickerty pickerty pie-sel-ickerty
Pompa lori jig
Every man that has no hair
Generally wears a wig
One two three, out goes he
Ickerty pickerty pie-sel-ickerty
Pompa lori jig
Edinburgh, Rymour, 1911

Iggoty piggoty
Iso liggity
Umpah pygo jig
Every man in China
Ought to wear a wig
Bellahouston, Glasgow, 1960s/70s

Ippitty soopitty, ippetty sap
Ippetty soopitty cunella cunapp
Cunellow up, cunellow down
Cunellow into Chinatown
Aberdeen, Lomax, 1951

I've a cherry, I've a chess
I've a bonny blue glass
I've a dog amang the corn
Bah, Willie Buckhorn
Chambers, 1842

Last night as I lay on my pillow
Last night as I lay on my bed
I stuck my feet out of the window
In the morning the neighbours were dead
Glasgow, 1960s/70s

Let your whiskers grow
Let your whiskers grow
What's the use of trying?
Pull them out by the roots
Make laces for your boots
And look at all the money you'll be saving
Glasgow, 1960s/70s

Mary at the cottage door
Eating cherries off a plate
Doon fell the summer seat
I've a kistie, I've a creel
I've a barrelie fu o meal
To ser my bairnies till't be done
Come teetle, come tottle, come twenty-one
Forfar, 1948

My hert's in the Heilins, my claes is in the pawn
And my wife's awa to Paisley wi anither wife's man
Rymour, 1919

My ship's home from China
With a cargo of tea
All laden with presents for you and me
She brought me one fan
Just think of my bliss
I fan myself daily like this, like this
Temple, Glasgow, 1960s/70s

Naebody likes me, everybody hates me
Think I'll go and eat worms
Big fat juicy ones, wee thin skooshy ones
See how they wriggle and squirm
Cut off their heads, squeeze out the juice
And throw the skins away
Nobody knows how I survive
On worms three times a day
Pollokshields, Glasgow, 1960s/70s

Nievie-nievie nick-nack
Which hand will ye tak?
Tak the right, tak the wrang
I'll beguile ye if I can
Chambers, 1842

Once upon a time
When the pigs spoke rhyme
And the monkeys chewed tobacco
And the hens took snuff
To make them tough
And ducks went quack quack quack-oh
Forfar, 1948

One's nane, two's some
Three's a pickle, four's a pund
Five's a dainty, six is plenty
Seven's a horse's meal
Argyllshire, 1901

Pease brose and barley-o, barley-o, barley-o
Pease brose and barley-o
Sugary cakes and candy
Glasgow, 1960s/70s

Puir wee ragged laddie runnin doon the street
Greetin fur his mammy in his wee bare feet
Greetin wi the cauld, shiverin wi the rain
Puir wee ragged laddie, he's a drunken cairter's wean
Rottenrow, Glasgow, 1960s/70s

Ree-a-ree a ranigate, the pipers i' the Canigate
The drow is in the air
The cock craws, the hen lays
The nicht afore the fair
Rymour, 1911

Salvation Army free from sin
Went to heaven in a corn mutton tin
The corn mutton tin began to smell
Salvation Army went to hell
Glasgow, 1960s/70s

Sleepy Dukie sits i the neukie
Canna win oot to play
The drums 'ill beat an the pipes 'ill play
The cocks 'ill craw and the hens 'ill lay
An the morn's the merry merry market day
MacLennan, 1909

The morn's the market and I'll be there
Kissin my lad and gettin my fair
The cocks'll be crawin and the hen'll be layin
For the morn's the merry merry Market Day
Forfar, 1948

There's a party on the hill
Would you like to come
With your own cream face
And your own cream bun?
Who is your true love?
[name] will be there
With her knickers on her hair
Singing aye aye ippy ippy out
Dalkeith, 1997

Three cheers for the red, white and blue
It sticks to your nose like glue
You laugh and you laugh
And you canna get it aff
Three cheers for the red, white and blue
Forfar, 1948

Three wee sausages
Frying in a pan
One popped out
And the other said 'Scram'
Glasgow, 1960s/70s

Up a bogie lane
Ta buy a penny whistle
The bogie man came up to me
An stole ma penny whistle
I asked him fur it back
He said he hudny got it
Ha ha ha, hee hee hee
I see it in your pocket
Glasgow, 1993

When I was young I had no sense
I thought I'd go to sea
I stepped upon a Chinaman's ship
And the Chinaman said to me
Up skalla doon skalla
Back skalla roon skalla
That's what the Chinaman said to me
Glasgow, 1986

Where are you going, Mrs McGinty?
I'm going to see Brother John
And who's Brother John, Mrs McGinty?
The man that keeps the pawn
Bellahouston, Glasgow, 1960s/70s

Whether would you raither
Or raither would you whether
A soo's snoot stewed
Or a stewed soo's snoot?
Forfar, 1948

Found a Peanut

Found a peanut, found a peanut
Found a peanut just now
Found a peanut, found a peanut
Just now, just now

Going to eat it

Got a pain

Ring the doctor

'Pendicitis

Rip her open

No more peanuts

Couldnae find it

Went to heaven

Didnae like it

Went below

Saw ye's aa there
Bellahouston, Glasgow, 1960s/70s

HALLOWEEN A NICHT AT EEN

Halloween, a nicht at een, a canle and a custock
Doon Dons has got a wean, they ca it Bessie Aitken

Some ca't a kittlin, some ca't a cat
Some ca't a wee wean wi a straw hat

It gaed to its grannie's, to seek a wee bit breid
The grannie took the ladle and brak it owre its head

Oh, says the mither o't, my wean's deid
Oh, says the faither o't, never you heed

Gang oot by the back door, in by the tither
Through amang the green kail, you'll sune get anither
Calder Ironworks, Glasgow, Rymour, 1911

I Went to a Chinese Restaurant

Fun and Stories

I went to a Chinese restaurant, to buy
    a loaf of bread
He wrapped it up in a five-pound note and
    this is what it said

My name is Elvis Presley, I'm a movie star
I do the hippy hippy shakey and I play the guitar

The boys are hunky and the girls are sexy
Sittin in the back street, drinkin Pepsi

Where's yer faither? Roun the corner
In the harbour drinkin lager
He feels a bit dizzy and he draps doon deid
Glasgow, 1994

I went to a Chinese restaurant
To buy a loaf of bread bread bread

They wrapped it up in a five-pound note
And this is what I said said said

My name is Ina Wina
I come from China
Do us a favour
Push off
Erskine, 1992

I went to a Chinese restaurant
To buy a loaf of bread

They wrapped it up in a five-pound note
And this is what it said

My name is Ella Bella
Chicken chop chella
Chinese chopsticks, Indian fella
Whrooooooo, How!
Moray, 2006

I went to a Chinese restaurant
To buy a loaf of bread

He wrapped it up in a five-pound note
And this is what he said:

'My name is Ella-Bella-Cheeky-Fella-Chinese-
Chopsticks-Indian-Feathers-Woo-Woo-Pow!'
Glasgow, 1960s/70s

I went to a Chinese restaurant
To buy a loaf of bread

I wrapped it up in a five-pound note
And this is what I said

My name is Ellie Ellie
Chickalie chickalie
Um pum poodle, silly willy noodle
Chinese chopsticks, Indian cheddar
Huff Puff Wow
Moray, 2006

I went to a Chinese restaurant
To buy a loaf of bread

He wrapped it up in a ten-pound note
And this is what it said

My name is Andy Pandy
Sugary candy
Roly-poly, chocolate dip

I can do the can-can, I can do the splits
I can do the hula hoop just like this

Bow to the king, push to the queen
Show your knickers to the football team

Gonny hypnotise you, paralyse you
Turn around and shoot
Livingston, 2007

I went to a Chinese restaurant
To buy a loaf of bread

The lady gave me a five-pound note
And this is what I said

My name is Elvis Presley
Girls are sexy

Sitting in the back seat
Drinking Pepsi

Having a baby

In the Royal Navy

Boys go [kiss kiss]
Girls go wooooo
Dalkeith, 1997

ON TOP OF SPAGHETTI

On top of spaghetti, all covered in cheese
I lost my poor meatball when somebody sneezed

It rolled off the table and onto the floor
Then my poor meatball rolled out of the door

It rolled off the doorstep and onto the mat
Along came my father and the meatball went splat

It rolled in the garden and under a bush
And then my poor meatball was nothing but moosh

It went up to heaven on the Meatball Express
And my poor spaghetti was one meatball less
Erskine and Glasgow, 1990s

SEE SEE

See see my best friend
I cannot play with you
My dolly's got the flu
Chicken pops and measles too
Swing on my drainpipe
Slide down my cellar door
And we'll be jolly friends
For ever more
Glasgow, 1991

See see my playmate
I cannot play with you
My dolly's got the flu
So I flushed her down the loo
But now I'm older
I do not play with dolls
I play with B-O-Y-S
B-O-Y-S, boys, wow
Dalkeith, 1997

See see my playmate
Come out and play with me
We'll bring our dollies
And climb the apple tree
Slide down my rainbow
Into my sailing ship
We'll be friends for ever more
Dalkeith, 1997

See see oh play me
Come out and play with me
And bring your dollies too
Ah oo ah oo ah oo
Slide down the drainpipe
And through the sailor's door
And we'll be jolly friends
For ever more, shut that door
Bankton, Livingston, 2007

When I Was a Wee Thing

When I was a wee thing
'Bout six or seven year auld
I had no worth a petticoat
To keep me frae the cauld

Then I went to Edinburgh
To bonnie burrows town
And there I coft a petticoat
A kirtle, and a gown

As I cam hame again
I thought I wad big a kirk
And aa the fowls o the air
Wad help me to work

The heron, wi her lang neb
She moupit me the stanes
The doo, wi her rough legs
She led me them hame

The gled he was a wily thief
He rackled up the waa
The pyat was a cursed thief
She dang down aa

The hare came hirpling owre the knowe
To ring the morning bell
The hurcheon she came after
And said she wad do't hersel

The herring was the high priest
The salmon was the clerk
The howlet read the order
They held a bonnie wark
Chambers, 1842

WHEN SUZIE WAS A BABY

When Suzie was a baby
A baby Suzie was
She went a goo goo
A goo goo goo

When Suzie was a toddler
She went a walk walk
A walk walk walk

When Suzie was a schoolgirl
She went a 'Please, miss,
I can't do this'

When Suzie was a teenager
She went a 'Oo Ah, ah lost ma bra
Ah left ma knickers in ma boyfriend's car'

When Suzie was a mother
She went a 'Shoo shoo
A shoo shoo shoo'

When Suzie was a grannie
She went a 'Knit, knit
I lost my stitch'

When Suzie was a dead
A dead Suzie was
She went [silence]
Glenrothes, 1981

When Suzie was a child, she went
Miss, miss, I need a piss

When Suzie was an adult, she went
Smack smack, a smack smack smack

When Suzie was a ghost
She went whoo whoo, a whoo whoo whoo
Dalkeith, 1997

LADIES IN THE TIGHT SKIRTS CAN'T DO THIS

Movement and dance

A keppie, a clappie, a furlie-ma-jockie
Heel, toe, through you go
Salute to the king, bow to the queen
An turn your back on the Kaiser
Aberdeenshire, Wilson, 1993

Early in the morning
Past eight o'clock
You should hear the postman knock
Up jumps Jane running to the door
To catch a one-a-letter, two-a-letter
Three-a-letter, four
Rottenrow, Glasgow, 1960s/70s

Here comes Mrs Macaroni
Ridin on a pretty pony
Ridin through her house-aroanie
This is Katie's washing day
Rump stump, stoodle addie
Rump stump, stoodle addie
Rump stump, stoodle addie
This is Katie's washing day
Montrose, 1976, SSS

Hokey cokey, penny the lump
The mair ye ate, the mair ye jump
The mair ye jump, ye're sure tae faa
Hokey cokey, that's it aa
Lossiemouth, 2006

Hot peas and barley o, barley o, barley o
Hot peas and barley o, sugary cakes and candy
Glasgow, 1960s/70s

I am a Girl Guide dressed in blue
See all the actions I can do
Stand up at ease, bend your knees
Salute to the king, bow to the queen
Show your knickers to the football team
Glasgow, 1993

I lost my leg in the army
I found it in the navy
Dipped it in some gravy
And had it for my tea
Glasgow, 1960s/70s

I met a little Spanish girl called I C Tiara
And all the boys on the football pitch said I See Tiara
How's your boyfriend? All right
Died in the fish shop last night
What wis he eatin? Raw fish
How did he end up? Like this
Boghall, Bathgate, 2007

I paula tay paula tasca
Paulatay, paula toe
I paula tay paula tasca
Paulatay, paula toe
O alla tinka, to do the rhumba
Paulatay, paula toe
O alla tinka, to do the
Rhumba umba umba umba ay
Edinburgh, Lomax, 1951

I was going to the country
I was going to the fair
I met a senorita with a curl in her hair
Oh, shake it senorita
Shake it all you can
Rumble to the bottom
Rumble to the top
Turn around till you make a stop
Glasgow, 1991

Ladies in the tight skirts can't do this
Can't do this, can't do this
Ladies in the tight skirts can't do this
Can't do this
Rottenrow, Glasgow, 1960s / 70s

My Aunty Anna plays the pianna
24 hours a day
Do the splits
My Uncle Ryan keeps on cryin
24 hours a day
Do the splits
Moray, 2006

My name is
High low chucalow
Chucalow high low
High low chucalow
Chucalow high
Dalkeith, 1997

My name is MacNamara
I'm the leader of the band
My wife is Betty Grable
She's the fairest in the land
Oh she can dance, she can sing
And she can show her legs
The only thing she cannae dae
Is fry ham and eggs
Pollokshields, Glasgow, 1960s/70s

Nelson in the army, lost one arm
Nelson in the army, lost the other arm
Nelson in the army, lost one eye
Nelson in the army, lost the other eye
Nelson in the army, lost one leg
Nelson in the army, fell down dead
Glasgow, 1960s/70s

Not last night but the night before
Twenty-five robbers came to my door
As they walked out they said to me
Spanish dancers turn around
Spanish dancers touch the ground
Spanish dancers do the high kicks
Spanish dancers do the high splits
East End, Glasgow, 1997

Off the carpet, two and out
Miss a beat and you are out
I like coffee, I like tea
I like sitting on Cheyenne's knee
Rottenrow, Glasgow, 1960s/70s

Oh, what a little short shirt you've got
You'd better pull down the blind
Bellahouston, Glasgow, 1960s / 70s

Oliver Twist, you can't do this
So what's the use of trying
Number 1 touch your tongue
Number 2 touch your shoe
Number 3 touch your knee
Number 4 touch the floor
Number 5 take a dive
Number 6 do the splits
Rottenrow, Glasgow, 1960s / 70s

Om pom pay bonnalay, bonna lassie
Om pom pay bonnalay
Academic so funny
Academic puff puff
Whitdale, 1994

On the mountain stands a lady
Who she is I do not know
All she wants is gold and silver
All she wants is a nice young man
Rottenrow, Glasgow, 1960s / 70s

On the mountain stands a castle
And the owner Frankenstein
And his daughter Pansy Potter
She's my only Valentine
So I call on Linda dear
Linda dear, Linda dear
So I call on Linda dear
And out pops Jane till the next New Year
Rottenrow, Glasgow, 1960s / 70s

Pepsi-Cola, Pepsi-Cola
Irn-Bru, Irn-Bru
Boys have got the muscles
Teacher's got the brains
Girls have got the sexy legs
So we won the game [or 'And you've got nane']
I'm gonna hypnotise you
Paralyse you
Turn around and faint
Dalkeith, 1997

PK penny packet
First you chew it, then you crack it
Then you stick it on your jacket
PK, penny packet
Aberdeen, Lomax, 1951

A B C Together

A B C together, up together, down together
Back to front, heel to toe
Wiggle your bum and round you go
A B C, hit it

That's the way uh uh, I like it uh uh
That's the way uh uh, I like it uh uh
Pull the chain and start again

Boys got the muscles, teacher canny count
Girls have got the sexy legs, you better watch out
Hypnotise you, paralyse you, until you faint
East Calder, 2007

A Girl From France

There came a girl from France
There came a girl from Spain
There came a girl from USA
And this is how she came

Knees up, Mother Brown
Knees up, Mother Brown
Knees up, knees up
Don't get the breeze up
Knees up, Mother Brown

Hoppy on one shoe
Hoppy on one shoe
Hoppy hoppy, never stoppy
Hoppy on one shoe

Birly birly round [etc.]

Touchy touch the ground [etc.]
Campbeltown, 1956, SSS

Down Down Baby

Down down baby
Down by the roller coaster
Sweet sweet baby
I'll never let you go
Shoomy shoomy coco pop
Shoomy pow
Shoomy shoomy coco pop
Shoomy shoomy pow

Grandma, grandma, sick in bed
She called for the doctor and the doctor said

Let's get the rhythm of the head
Ding dong
Let's get the rhythm of the head
Ding dong
Let's get the rhythm of the hands
Clap clap
Let's get the rhythm of the hands
Clap clap
Let's get the rhythm of the feet
Stomp stomp
Let's get the rhythm of the feet
Stomp stomp
Get the rhythm of the ho-o-o-o-t dog

Put them all together and what dae ye get?
Ding dong, clap clap, stomp stomp, ho-o-o-o-t dog

Put them all backwards and what do you get?
Dog hot, stomp stomp, clap clap, dong ding

My old granny sleeps in bed
This is what the doctor said
She'll be all right in a week or two
No more school for me, just you
Dalkeith, 1997

I Have a Bonnet

I have a bonnet trimmed with blue
Do you wear it? Yes I do
I always wear it when I can
Going to the ball with my young man

My young man has gone to sea
When he comes back he will marry me
Tip to the heel and tip to the toe
That's the way the polka goes
Glasgow, 1986

Jelly on the Plate

Jelly on the plate, jelly on the plate
Wiggle waggle, wiggle waggle
Jelly on the plate

Sausage on the pan, sausage on the pan
Turn them over, turn them over
Sausage on the pan

Baby on the floor, baby on the floor
Pick him up, pick him up
Baby on the floor

Ghostie in the house, ghostie in the house
Kick him out, kick him out
Ghostie in the house

Apples on the tree, apples on the tree
Pull them off, pull them off
Apples on the tree
Aberdeen, 1951

LITTLE BUBBLE CAR

Ah had a little bumper car
Number 48
Ah took it round the coooooorner
And then ah pult ma brake
I had a little bubble car, Number 48
Turned it round the corner
And crashed it through a gate
Glasgow, 1960s/70s

I'm a little bubble car, number 48
I raced round the coooooorner and pressed on my brakes
How many miles can the bubble car go
5, 10, 15, 20
Moray, 2006

RONALD DONALD

Ronald Donald deshca peshca
Ronald Donald deshca peshca
I've got a boyfriend peshca
He's so sweet peshca
Sweeter than a cherry tree peshca
Ice-cream soda with the cherry on the top
Ice-cream soda with the cherry on the top

Down down baby, down by the roller coaster
Sweet sweet baby, I will never let you go
Shimmy shimmy coco pops
Shimmy shimmy I
Shimmy shimmy coco pops
Shimmy shimmy I
Bankhead, 1992

Teddy Bear

Teddy bear, teddy bear
Touch the ground
Teddy bear, teddy bear
Birl around

Teddy bear, teddy bear
Show your shoe
Teddy bear, teddy bear
That will do

Teddy bear, teddy bear
Run upstairs
Teddy bear, teddy bear
Say night prayers

Teddy bear, teddy bear
Switch off the light
Teddy bear, teddy bear
Say goodnight
Goodnight, teddy bear
Campbeltown, 1956, SSS

THE OLD GREY MARE

The old grey mare, she ain't what she used to be
Ain't what she used to be, ain't what she used to be
The old grey mare, she ain't what she used to be
Ever since the old man died – paralysed

The old grey mare she cannae dae a birlio

The old grey mare she cannae dae a jibbio
Rottenrow, Glasgow, 1960s/70s

UP AND DOWN THE HOOSE

Up and down the hoose
To buy a mickey moose
If you catch it by the tail
Hang it up on a rusty nail

Send for the cook
To make a bowl of soup
Hurrah boys hurrah
How do you like ma soup?

I like it very well
Apart fae the smell
Kings and queens and jellybeans
We all jump out
Glasgow, 1960s/70s and 1993

IF YOU HIT THE ONE WEE MOLL

Trouble and strife

Ah wish ah hud a penny
Tae buy a penny gun
Ah'd pit it on ma shouder
An ah'd mak the bobby run
Moray, 2006

Aw maw, I got an awfy hammerin
Who fae? Wee Geordie Cameron
Whit fur? Because I wouldnae marry him
I'll tell the polis in the morning
Rottenrow, Glasgow, 1960s/70s

Here lies my Barbie doll
Pretty pink and dead
My horrid little brother's
Just blown off her head
Moray, 2006

I place my hand upon your head
Now a thousand bugs are dead
Glasgow, 1960s/70s

I ring I ring a pinky
If I tell a lee
I'll gang tae the bad place
Whenever I dee
White pan, black pan
Burn me tae death
Tak a muckle gully
An cut ma breath
Ten miles below the earth
Hendry & Stephen, 1978

I want ma butter
I want ma butter, ma sugar, ma tea
Waiting at the Maypole door
I don't want to get the flu
Staunin in a queue
I want ma butter, ma sugar, ma tea
Glasgow, 1960s/70s

Little fattie policeman don't blame me
Blame that boy behind that tree
He stole sugar, he stole tea
Policeman, policeman don't blame me
Rottenrow, Glasgow, 1960s/70s

Mary Ellen I'm no playin
Cos there's nae chap-chapsies
In this game
You get chapsies, I get nane
So Mary Ellen I'm no playin
Rottenrow, Glasgow, 1960s/70s

Murder murder polis, three stair up
The wumman in the middle flat hit me wi a cup
Ma heid's aa achin, ma lip's aa cut
Murder murder polis, three stair up
Glasgow, 1960s/70s

One fine day in the middle of the night
Two dead men got up to fight
One blind man to see fair play
Another dumb man to shout hurray
Up came a nanny goat and knocked them
    through a nine-inch wall
Into a dry ditch that drowned them all
Forfar, 1948

Ride awa to Aberdeen and buy white breid
But lang ere she cam back again,
    the carlin she was deid
He up wi his muckle club, and gied her in the heid
Fie, carlin, rise again and eat white breid
Edinburgh, Rymour, 1919

Roses are red
Violets are blue
A face like yours
Belongs in the zoo
Bellahouston, Glasgow, 1960s/70s

South of the border, down Germany way
There is a nasty bloke we'd love tae
    choke who dreams today
Of being the ruler of half the earth
We should have drowned him the day of his birth
Bellahouston, Glasgow, 1960s/70s

Tell tale tit
Your knickers will split
Your dad's in the dustbin
Eating fish and chips
Dalkeith, 1997

The Boys' Brigade, they are afraid
To stick their nose in marmalade
Rottenrow, Glasgow, 1960s/70s

There is a happy land, doon in Duke Street jail
Where aa the prisoners stand tied tae a nail
Ham-and-eggs we never see, dirty water fur yer tea
There we live in misery. God save the Queen
Glasgow, 1950s

There is a wee hoose ca'd Barlinnie, haw haw
Where ye drink yer tea frae a tinny, haw haw
The warders are there tae shave aff yer hair
In that lovely wee hoose ca'd Barlinnie
John Street, Glasgow, 1960s/70s

There she goes, there she goes
Peerie heels and pointie toes
Look at her feet, she thinks she's neat
Black stockins an dirty feet
West Lothian, 1990s

Tommy had a gun and the gun was loaded
Tommy pulled the trigger and the gun exploded
No more Tommy, no more gun
No more damage to be done
Rottenrow, Glasgow, 1960s/70s

Tommy Thistle blew a whistle
On a Sunday morning
The policeman came and took Tommy's name
And Tommy bowed good-morning
Rottenrow, Glasgow, 1960s / 70s

Under the old apple tree
An apple said to me
Apple pudding apple pie
Have you ever told a lie – NO
Yes you have, you stole your mother's teapot lid
What colour was it – GOLD
No it wasn't, it was silver
That's another lie you told
Bellahouston, Glasgow, 1960s / 70s

Vote vote vote for Campbell Stephen
Vote vote vote for aa his men
And we'll buy a penny gun
And we'll make the Germans run
And we'll never see the Germans any more
Glasgow, 1958

Vote vote vote for Mr Churchill
Who's that knocking at the door
If it's Hitler and his wife
Take a poker and a knife
And we won't see Hitler any more
Shut the door
Bellahouston, Glasgow, 1960s / 70s

Way down upon the Swanee River
Where I fell in with a splash
Along came an alligator singing
Britannia, Britannia, ma maw's making jam
Chinese sausages and Belfast ham
Glasgow, 1960s/70s

Whau'll buy me Jockey-be-laund?
Wat an he dees ata me haund?
De back sall bear da seddle-baund
Troo moss and mire, troo barn and byre
Owre stocks and stanes, an deed men's banes
An au sall lie upo dy back and anes
If do lets me janty Jockey edder dee or fa
Shetland, Saxby, 1932

AUNTIE MARY AND BARNUM AND BAYLEY

Auntie Mary had a canary
Up the leg o her drawers
It whistled for oors an frightened the Boers
An won the Victoria Cross
Stonehouse, 1992

Auntie Mary had a canary
Up the leg o her drawers
It pulled a string and began tae sing
And doon fell Santa Claus
Maryhill, Glasgow, 1950s

Barnum and Bayley
Had a canary
Whustled 'The Cock o the North'
It whustled for oors
An frichtened the Booers
An they aa fell intae the Forth

B for Booer
K for Krudger
J for General French
The Bri'ish were up at the tap o the hull
An the Booers were doon in the trench
Shelmerdine, 1932

I HAD THE GERMAN MEASLES

I had the German measles
I had them very bad
They threw me in an ambulance
And took me in a cab

The cab was very bumpy
I nearly fell out
And when I got to the hospital
I heard a baby shout

Mammy, daddy, take me home
I've been here a week or two
Here comes Doctor Alistair
Slidin down the bannister

Halfway down he ripped his pants
Now he's doin the cha cha dance
Cha cha cha cha cha cha cha
Cha cha cha cha cha cha cha
Glasgow, 1992

Last Night There Was a Murder

Last night there was a murder in the chip shop
A wee dug stole a haddy bone
A big dug tried tae take it aff him
So ah hit it wi a tattie scone

Ah went roon tae see ma Aunty Sarah
Bit ma Aunty Sarah wisnae in
So I keeked through a hole in the windae
And ah shouted 'Aunty Sarah, are ye in?'

Her false teeth were lyin on the table
Her curly wig wis lyin on the bed
An ah laughed an ah laughed till ma heid fell aff
When ah saw her screwing aff her wudden leg
Glasgow, 1950s

Nellie McSwiggan

Nellie McSwiggan got tossed oot the jiggin
For liftin her leg too high
All of a sudden a big black puddin
Came flyin through the air

Oh wha saw the kilties comin
Wha saw them gang awa
Wha saw the kilties comin
Sailin doon the Broomielaw

Some o them had tartan troosers
Some o them had nane at a
Some o them had tartan troosers
Sailin doon the Broomielaw
Glasgow, 1986

NINE IN THE BED

Please remember to tie a knot in your pyjamas
Single beds are only meant for
1, 2, 3, 4, 5, 6, 7, 8
Nine in the bed and the little one said
'Roll over, roll over'
So they all rolled over and one fell out
And banged his head and began to shout

Please remember to tie a knot in your pyjamas
Single beds are only meant for
1, 2, 3, 4, 5, 6, 7
Eight in the bed and the little one said
'Roll over, roll over' [etc.]
Glenrothes, 1981

NOSES IN THE BUTTER

Today is Hogmanay, tomorrow's Hogmananny
And ah'm gaun up the brae, tae see ma Irish grannie
Ah'll take her tae a ball, ah'll take her tae a supper
And when ah get her there ah'll stick her nose in the butter
Singin ah ah ah ah ah, ah ah ah ah ah ah
Ah, ah ah ah ah, and that's the Gaelic chorus
Kilbarchan and Plean, 1920s

The nicht's Hogmanay
The morn's Hogmanay
Far across the sea
Tae see my Susannay

Some fowks says I'm daft
Some fowks says I'm crackit
Offer me half-a-croon
And see if I'll no tak it

I took her tae a ball
And took her tae a supper
She fell ower the table
And stuck her nib ee butter
Forfar, 1948

My uncle died a week ago, he left me all his riches
A wooden leg, a feather bed, a pair of leather breeches
A tobacco box without a lid, a jug without a handle
A coffee pot without a spout, and half of a farthing candle

I travelled east, I travelled west, I came to Alabama
I fell in love with a nice young girl, her name was
    Susy Anna
I took her to the ball one night, and also to the supper
The table fell, and she fell too, and stuck her nose
    in the butter
Rymour, 1919

Away down east, away down west
Away down Alabama
The only girl that I love best
Her name is Susy Anna

I took her to a ball one night
And sat her down to supper
The table fell and she fell too
And stuck her nose in butter

The butter, the butter
The holy margarine
Two black eyes and a jelly nose
And the rest all painted green
Edinburgh, Ritchie, 1964

Three wee wives and three wee wives and three
    wee wives make nine
Says your wee wife tae my wee wife, 'Will ye lend me
    ma washin line?'
Says my wee wife to your wee wife, 'When will ah
    get it back?'
Says your wee wife to ma wee wife, 'Ah'll skelp yer
    humphy back'
Oh didn't we laugh, oh didn't we laugh tae skelp her
    humphy back

Didn't we laugh, oh didn't we laugh tae skelp her
    humphy back
I hunted east, I hunted west, I hunted Alabama
The only girl that I could find was bonny Susy Anna
I took her to the ball one night, set her down to supper
The table fell and she did yell and stuck her
    nose in the butter
Oh didn't we laugh, oh didn't we laugh tae see her
    nose in the butter
Didn't we laugh, oh didn't we laugh tae see her
    nose in the butter
The butter, the butter, the holy margarine
Twa black eyes and a jelly nose and her face aa
    paintit green

Her faither died twa weeks ago, left her aa his riches
A feather bed, a corky leg, and twa three broken crutches
Oh didn't we laugh, oh didn't we laugh tae see her
    broken crutches
Didn't we laugh, oh didn't we laugh tae see her
    broken crutches
Glenrothes, 2003

TAKE A TRAMCAR

Take a tramcar, take a trolley
Take a bus to George's Square
There you'll see a famous Orangeman
Sitting on his big white mare
He is William Prince of Orange
And no Fenian can deny
That he slew the Fenian army
On the twelfth day of July
Glasgow, 1960s/70s

If you want to see King William
Take your trumpet to the Cross
There you'll see a noble lady
Riding on a big black horse
Riddle doodle, deedle daddle
Riding on a big black horse
Argyllshire, 1901

The Day I Went to Sea

When I was one I sucked my thumb
The day I went to sea
I jumped upon a pirate's ship
And the captain said to me
'We're going this way, that way
Forward and back way
Over the deep blue sea
A bottle of rum to fill my tum
And that's the life for me'

When I was two I tied my shoe

When I was three I skelpt my knee

When I was four I shut the door

When I was five I did a dive

When I was six I did the splits

When I was seven I went to heaven

When I was eight I shut the gate

When I was nine I broke my spine

When I was ten I started again
Glasgow, 1992

THE LUCKENBOOTHS

As I went by the Luckenbooths I saw a lady fair
She had long pendles in her ears and jewels in her hair
And when she cam to oor door she spiered at wha was ben
'Oh, hae ye seen my lost love wi his braw Hieland men?'

The smile upon her bonnie cheek was sweeter than the bee
Her voice was like the birdie's sang upon the birken tree
But when the meenister cam out her mare began to prance
Then rade into the sunset beyond the coast of France
Edinburgh, Moffat, 1933

THE NIGHT WAS DARK

The night was dark, the war was over
Battlefields were covered in blood
There I spied a wounded soldier
Lying dying saying these words

God bless my home in bonny Scotland
God bless my wife and only child
God bless the men who died for Scotland
Holding up the Union Jack
Glasgow, 1960s / 70s

The Quartermaster's Store

There was gravy, gravy that sunk
    the German navy
In the store, in the store
There was gravy, gravy that sunk
    the German navy
In the quartermaster's store

My hands are sore, I cannot fight
I got the teacher's strap last night
Glasgow and Dingwall, 1950s

We Are the Boys

We are the Scurvy boys
We make a lot of noise
We wear our trousers to our knees
We never smoke or drink
That's what our mothers think
We are the Temple Scurvy boys
Temple, Glasgow, 1960s/70s

We are the Rab boys
We make a lot of noise
We wear our trousers to our knees,
    to our knees
What do our parents say
When we go out to play
We are the super Rab boys
East End, Glasgow, 1991

We Are the Girls

We are the Rothesay girls
We wear our hair in curls
We wear our dungarees
Below our sexy knees

My daddy was surprised
Tae see ma belly rise
My mammy jumped for joy
Tae see a baby boy
Bute, 1994

We are the bovver girls
We wear our hair in curls
We wear our dungarees
To just below our knees

We wear our fathers' suits
We wear our brothers' ties
And if we want a guy
We simply wink one eye

The boy next door
He had me on the floor
My mother was surprised
To see my belly rise

My father jumped with joy
To see a baby boy
We are the bovver girls
From Scurvy-Land
Glasgow, 1960s/70s

We are the gypsy girls
We got our hair in curls
We got our dangarees upon our sexy knees

We wear our bras so tight
Show we can fight
We are the gypsy girls
Moray, 2006

WEE GALLUS BLOKES AND MOLLS

Oh, yir ma wee gallus bloke nae mair
Oh, yir ma wee gallus bloke nae mair
Wi yir bell-blue strides an yer bunnet tae the side
Oh, yir ma wee gallus bloke nae mair

When I went by the sweetie works, ma hert begun tae beat
Saw aa the herry pie walkin doon the street
Wi their flashy, dashy petticoats, flashy, dashy shawls
Their five an tanner gutty boots, oh we're big gallus molls

As I came by the dancin, I began tae think
Will aa the lassies stand and talk aboot oor Jeanie's mink
Or will they hae a na'er wi me aboot ma past
But just as I came up to them they walked away right fast
Glasgow, 1957, SSS and Glasgow, 1960s

For we are three wee Glesga molls, we kin let you see
An if you hit the one wee moll, ye'll hae tae hit the three
Flashy dashy petticoats, flashy dashy shawls
Twelve an a tanner's worth o boots, an we're the gallus molls
Aberdeen, 1960, SSS

Oh, we are three wee gallus girls sailing on the sea
And if you pick the fairest one, the fairest one shall be
Oh, rasha tasha petticoat, rasha tasha tee
Rasha tasha petticoat, the fairest one shall be
Moss Park, Glasgow, 1961

WHO SHAVED THE BARBER?

Who shaved the barber, the barber, the barber?
Who shaved the barber?
The barber shaved himself

Who put on his waistcoat, his waistcoat, his waistcoat?
Who put on his waistcoat?
He put it on himself

Catch him by the waistcoat
The jaicket, the overcoat
Tell him he's a billygoat
And throw him doon the stairs
Glasgow, 1986

THE BALDIE HEIDED MASTER
School life

Bill and Ben flowerpot men
Went to school at half-past ten
The teacher says you're late again
Bill and Ben flowerpot men
Rottenrow, 1960s/70s

Doctor Faustus was a good man
He whipped his scholars now and then
When he whipped them, he made them dance
Out of Scotland into France
Out of France into Spain
And then he whipped them back again
Chambers, 1842

From the hills of Pinkston Drive
To the shores of Bubble-gum Bay
We will fight the caretaker
With stink bombs, mud and clay
We will fight him for the glory
We will fight him round the bend
We will fight him for the fun
We will fight him to the end
Glasgow, 1960s/70s

Hi ho, hi ho, it's off to school we go
Wi a bucket and a spade and a hand grenade
Hi ho, hi ho
Hi ho, hi ho, it's off to school we go
It's yap yap yap, and we get the strap
Hi ho, hi ho
East Milton, East Kilbride, 1960s/70s

Master Foster very good man
Sweeps his college now and than
After that he takes a dance
Up from London down to France
With a black bonnet and a white snout
Stand ye there for ye are out
Chambers, 1842

Mine eyes have seen the glory
Of the burning of the school
We have tortured every teacher
We have broken every rule
Down with education and up with liberation
The school is burning down
Glasgow, 1991

My teacher's barmy
My teacher's barmy
She wears a tammy
She joined the army
When she was 1, 2, 3, 4, 5
Temple, Glasgow, 1960s/70s

No more English, no more French
No more sitting on the old school bench
Teacher, teacher I declare
I can see your underwear
Is it black? Is it white?
Oh my god, it's dynamite
Dalkeith, 1997

Off to school, off to school
Pass your 'quali' and that's the rule
You silly wee ass, you couldnae pass
Now John Smith is the bottom of the class
Rottenrow, Glasgow, 1960s/70s

Oor teacher's a smasher
A face like a tattie masher
A nose like a pickled onion
And eyes like green peas
Glasgow, 1960s/70s

Robin Hood and his merry men
Went to school at half-past ten
Teacher said you're late again
Robin Hood and his merry men
Glasgow, 1960s/70s

School dinners, school dinners
Concrete chips, concrete chips
Dinner's on the wall, dinner's on the wall
I hate school, I hate school
Glasgow, 1960s/70s

Stop the bus ah need a wee wee
Stop the bus ah need a wee wee
Stop the bus ah need a wee wee
A wee wee cup o tea
Glenrothes, 1981

Teacher, teacher let me in
Ma feet's cauld, ma shin's thin
If ye dinna let me in
Ah'll no come back this aifternin
Dumfries, 1960

The bell, the bell, the B-I-L
Tell the teacher I'm no well
If you're late, shut the gate
And don't come back till half-past eight
Rottenrow, Glasgow, 1960s/70s

We break up, we break down
We don't care if the school falls down
No more English, no more French
No more sitting on the old school bench
If your teacher interferes
Knock her down and box her ears
If that does not serve her right
Blow her up with dynamite
Glasgow, 1991

COME TO OUR SCHOOL

Come to our school, come to our school
For a life of misery
There's a notice in the playground
Saying 'Welcome unto thee'

Don't believe it, don't believe it
It's a load of bloody lies
If it wasn't for the teachers
It would be a paradise

Build a bonfire, build a bonfire
Put the teachers on the top
Put the jannie in the middle
And burn the bloody lot
Whitburn, 1997

GLORY GLORY

Glory glory hallelujah
Teacher hit me wi a ruler
The ruler broke in two
And she hit me wi her shoe
And I went greetin hame

Glory glory hallelujah
Teacher hit me wi a ruler
I hit her on the seater
With a 45 repeater
And I've never saw the teacher any more
Glasgow, 1960s/70s

Glory glory hallelujah
The teacher hit me wi a ruler
Ah punched her in the belly
And she wobbled like a jelly
And she never came back to school

Glory glory hallelujah
The teacher hit me wi a ruler
The ruler broke in two
And she hit me with her shoe
And I went greetin hame
Glasgow, 1960s/70s

In Beechwood

They say that in Beechwood the food is mighty fine
A pea fell off the table and killed a pal of mine
Oh I don't want to be a Beechwood Bird
Gee boys, I wanna go home
(To see ma mammy)
Gee boys, I wanna go home

They say that in Beechwood the fags are mighty fine
You ask for twenty Regal, they gie ye five Woodbine

They say that in Beechwood the booze is mighty fine
You ask for Eldorado, they gie ye turpentine

They say that in Beechwood the beds are mighty fine
You jump on a pillow and nearly break your spine
Glasgow, 1960s/70s

Ma Wee School

Ma wee school's a braw wee school
It's made wi brick an plaster
The only thing that's wrang wi it
Is the baldie heided master

He gangs tae the pub on Saturday night
He gangs tae the kirk on Sunday
He prays tae God tae gie him strength
Tae ba'er the weans on Monday
Glenrothes, 1981

MURDER MIGHTY MURDER

Oh it's murder mighty murder in the hoose
When the cat he does the rhumba wi the moose
If ye hit him wi a poker
He'll dae the Carioca
It's murder mighty murder in the hoose

It's murder mighty murder in the school
When the teacher hits ye wi a widden rule
If ye canny dae yer grammar
She hits ye wi a hammer
It's murder mighty murder in the school

It's murder mighty murder in the school
It's murder mighty murder in the school
If ye canny dae yer spellin
She'll melt ye wi a mellan
It's murder mighty murder in the school

It's murder mighty murder in the jail
Where they feed ye breid and watter frae a pail
If ye ask them for a tinnie
They'll send ye tae Barlinnie
It's murder mighty murder in the jail
Glasgow, 1950s

OLD SMOKEY

On top of Old Smokey, all covered with sand
I shot my poor teacher with an elastic band

I shot her with pleasure, I shot her with pride
I couldn't have missed her, she's forty foot wide

I went to her funeral, I went to her grave
Some people threw flowers, I threw a grenade

I opened her grave, saw she wasn't quite dead
I got a bazooka, and blew off her head

A million wee pieces went up in the sky
And that was the first time my teacher could fly
Glasgow and Erskine, 1990s

On top of old Smokey, all covered in blood
There lives a poor vampire, stuck in the mud
An axe through his belly, a knife through his head
I came to the conclusion, the poor soul was dead
Blairdardie, Glasgow, 1960s/70s

SIXTEEN SUMS

Ye dae sixteen sums and what dae ye get?
Fifteen wrang and six of the belt
Teacher don't ye call me cause I can't come
Ah'm stuck tae ma seat wi bubbly-gum

If ye go to school dinners better leave them aside
A lot of kids didn't and a lot of kids died
The meat's made of iron, the totties of steel
And if that doesny get ye then the pudding will
Glasgow, 1960s / 70s

UNDER THE BRAMBLE BUSHES

Under the bramble bushes
Down by the sea
True love for you my darling
True love for me

When we get married
We'll have a family
A boy for you, a girl for me
How many fishes are in the sea?
Eleven and twelve makes twenty-three
That's the end of chapter three

Twelve and twelve makes twenty-four
Push your teacher out the door
If she says 'Don't do that'
Hit her on the head with a baseball bat

Row row row your boat
Gently down the stream
Push the teacher overboard
And listen to her scream
AAAAHHHH
Moray, 2006

I Sat on My Houtie Croutie

Memory tests and puzzles

These 'rigmaroles' were collected from adults who had learned them in childhood as feats of memory. Each set of words could be painstakingly unpacked to identify the elements of various rhymes about places, lines from or parodying popular songs, arcane references and unexplained puzzles – better just to admire what remarkable memories some folk have.

EERIE ORIE VIRGIN MARY

Eerie orie, Virgin Mary
Aa the keetles in a tearie
Tak up your fit and gie's a pu
Seven weeks have I been fu
Seven more shall I be
By the weeks of Marie
Marie an St John
Aa the tailors in the tron
Up the bank and doon the brae
Lang fit and short tae
Gie his tail to the pleuch
My tail's lang eneuch
Edinburgh, nineteenth century, GD

I'll Tell Ye a Tailie

I'll tell ye a tailie
Aboot the fit and the failie
And the brunt bridle o Killiemeer
That nae man weel feart
I took my fit in my hand
And I hit it owre to Ireland
And fat saw ye there?
I saw the maiden at the window
Kaimin her hair
And by cam the cock
And snappit the kaim fae 'er
And he took gate and she took gate
And throw the meer they ran
And fair fa ye Blue-breekies
Saw ye my guidman?
I saw your guidman
And I'll tell ye fu
He brunt a hole in's breeks
And fat maks that to you?
New Deer, GD

Jock, John, Jellie, Jam

Jock, John, Jellie, Jam, he cam linkin owre dam
Owre dam, owre dyke, trip o my taillie
Taillie and richt knot, dear bocht, dear saul
She keepit sheep o green faul
As sheep sae did she swine, they ca'd her faither Lord Lyne
Lord Lyne, tilly tackit, hairy hal his mither nakit
Mither nakit tho she be, tho a the limbs a limmer tee
Limmer tee, limmer ta, Jeannie Fyke stoo'd the tail fae my tyke
Rymour, 1911

MARY ANNIE

Mary Annie, sugar cannie
Bumbee bedlar
Saxteen saidler
A mannie in a hairy caipie
Rowin at the fairy boatie
Fairy boatie ow'r dear
Ten pounds in the year
Jock Fite had a coo
Black and white aboot the moo
Hit can jump the Brig o Dee
Singin Cock-a-linkie
Portsoy, 1902, SSS

THE CARLE SITS UPO THE SEA

The carle sits upo the sea
A his canles on his knee
Ye's three an I's fower
Shaw's the gate tae Aiberdour
Aiberdour an' Aiberdeen
Cragleith upo the green
Cragleith and Wullie Fair
Fat's gweed for a deer?
For a deer an a dog
Cam to warn Wullie Tod
Wullie Tod an Wullie Tey
They were baith born in May
Lunon is a hard gate
Quo the eel unto the skate
Quo the haddock to the eel
Crook ye your tail weel

As weel micht ye be
As the sheep o Lunnerty
Lunnerty an jeelie fike
Staw the rumples fae ma tyke
Fae ma tyke an fae ma turn
Gie me siller, gie me some
Gie me gowd, gie me nane
Ca ma mither Jerry King
Jerry King and Jerry Couth
Staw a pair o gingers
Ten pair o fite feet
Kent ye Thrumlie?
Thrumlie had a mear
Foo mony bags did she bear?
Ten an the monyfauld
Kent ye John Auld
John Auld and Jeelsie
Rang the bell o Dousie
Dousie and Dulzie
Happiky an Hulzie
Rotten geese an almond waters
Inverugie, GD

The Cobbling Grace

Aa ye married men tween threescore and ten
That dinna attend this cobblin'll be cobbled owre again
Wi the rug wi the pug wi the weel pu'd lug
That dog o Andro Morrison's he sits afore the pu'pit
Neeb neeb nabblin at his cods
He'll aither gar me lauch or stick the preachin
But ye can hund him up the lang lane or
        doon by Nellie Morrison's
Dinna miss a stroke but kill him if ye can
For he eatit aa Johnnie McFushie-ca'its peys
No only that he pished amon the strae
Which was a great sin
Ye hunder, ye dunder, ye great goose horn
Here a tift, there a tift, amang the laird's corn
An X and an E and an auld aipple tree
Whistle Jock and ye'll get free
North-East, Rymour, 1911

Yon Heich Heich Hill

As I gaed owre yon heich heich hill
To meet my father, he'd gane will
He had mony bonnie things

He'd a chillie, he'd a chase
He'd a bonnie blue gless
He'd a dog amon the corn
Blawin Billy Buck's horn

Billy Buck had a coo
Black and fite aboot the mou
They ca'd her Belly Bentie
And she lap owre the Brig o Dee
Like ony covilintie
New Pitsligo, GD

Where Is Humber Jumber?

As I went up by Humber Jumber
Humber Jumber jinny o
There I met a hokum pokum
Carrying off Capriny o
Oh, if I'd had my tit my tat
My tit my tat my tinny o
I would have made my hokum pokum
Lay me down Capriny o
Chambers, 1842

I sat upon me humpie birlie
An I lookit doon troo da humpie dirlie
An I saw the Ree-Raw
Cairryin da Lintie's pipes awa
An I swore be mi nittie nattie
That I wid tak mi wittie wattie
An mak the Ree-Raw
Pey for cairryin da Lintie's pipes awa
Shetland, Saxby, 1932

JERUSALEM RHYMES

I sat upon my houtie croutie
I lookit owre my rumple routie
And saw John Heezlum Peezlum
Playin on Jerusalem pipes
Argyllshire, 1901

Minty tinty halgulum
Mortal portal piel a gum
I saw the laird o Eastle Weastle
Jumpin owre Jerus'lum steeple
Rymour

Tootie tinty, henery memory
Bawptie leeritie, hover dover
Saw the King o Hale Pale
Gruppin at his cuddy's tail
Jumpin ower Jerusalem dykes
Playin on his wee bagpipes
One two three, oot goes he
Dumfriesshire, 1928

THE END

Noo my story's endit
And gin ye be offendit
Tak a needle and a threid
And sew a bit t' end o't
Forfar, 1948

Abbreviations and Sources

Aberdeen and Edinburgh, 1951, Lomax. Alan Lomax archive, Association for Cultural Equity, New York, USA.

Argyllshire, 1901. R C Maclagan, *The Games & Diversions of Argyleshire*. London, David Nutt for Folklore Society.

Buchan, 1962. Norman Buchan, *101 Scottish Songs*. Glasgow, Collins.

Castlemilk, late 1980s. *Ma Maw Says*, a cassette of singing by Castlemilk pensioners, issued by the WEA for Castlemilk People's History Group.

Chambers, 1842. Robert Chambers, *Popular Rhymes of Scotland*. Edinburgh, W & R Chambers.

Davison, 1960s/70s. Ian Davison, index of songs collected by him from Glasgow schoolchildren.

Forfar, 1948. Jean C Rodger, *'Lang Strang'*. Forfar Press.

Fraser, 1975. Amy S Fraser, *Dae Ye Min' Langsyne?* London, Routledge & Kegan Paul.

GD. Patrick Shuldham-Shaw, Emily Lyle & Katherine Campbell, *The Greig-Duncan Folk Song Collection,* Volume 8. Edinburgh, Mercat Press (2002). Texts of GD 1548, 1554, 1559, 1566B, 1567, 1575B, 1576, 1578B, 1583A, 1587, 1621, 1632, 1635, 1640B, 1642, 1644A, 1660, 1661, 1669B, 1691A, 1721C, part texts of GD 1373, 1634.

Various Glasgow areas, 1960s/70s. Ian Davison, index of songs collected by him from Glasgow schoolchildren.

Glasgow, 1986. Maureen Sinclair, *Murder Murder Polis*. Edinburgh, Ramsay Head Press.

Hendry & Stephen, 1978. I D Hendry & G Stephen, *Scotscape*. Edinburgh, Oliver & Boyd.

Hendry & Stephen, 1982. I D Hendry & G Stephen, *Scotsgate*. Edinburgh, Oliver & Boyd.

Herd, 1776. David Herd, *Ancient & Modern Scottish Songs*. Edinburgh, Scottish Academic Press (1973).

Lomax, 1951. Alan Lomax, *Singing in the Streets*. Rounder CD 82161-1795-2, issued in 2003.

MacLennan, 1909. R J MacLennan, *Scottish Nursery Rhymes*. London, Andrew Melrose.

Moffat, 1933. Alfred Moffat, *Fifty Traditional Scottish Nursery Rhymes*. London, Augener.

Ritchie, 1964. James T R Ritchie, *The Singing Street*. Edinburgh, Oliver & Boyd.

Ritchie, 1965. James T R Ritchie, *Golden City*. Edinburgh, Oliver & Boyd.

Rymour, various dates. *Miscellanea of the Rymour Club*. Published by the Club in parts from 1905 to 1928, and in three volumes in 1911, 1919, 1928, Edinburgh.

Saxby, 1932. Jessie M E Saxby, *Shetland Traditional Lore*. Edinburgh, Grant & Murray.

Shelmerdine, 1932. J M Shelmerdine & F Greirson. *Nicht At Eenie*. Warlingham, Samson Press.

SSS. The School of Scottish Studies Recordings archive, George Square, Edinburgh. From Henderson recordings SSS SA1954/139–42, SSS SA1956/171–2, SSS SA1957/99 SSS SA1960/241.

Dates from 1991 to 2006 are from the McVicar Collection of manuscripts and recordings from schoolchildren.

Full details of the above sources and all others used can be found in *Doh Ray Me, When Ah Wis Wee* by Ewan McVicar, Edinburgh, Birlinn (2007).

Acknowledgements

My grateful thanks are given to the following:

Staff at the School of Scottish Studies, University of Edinburgh, Ian Davison for the use of his manuscript collection, staff at the Association for Cultural Equity, New York, Tom Laurie, Pam Diamond, Susan Thores, Paul Snow. Head teachers, teachers and helpers, and especially pupils in many Scottish schools.

Particular thanks are due to the University of Aberdeen for permission to include a substantial number of texts from *The Greig-Duncan Folk Song Collection*, Volume 8, edited by Patrick Shuldham-Shaw, Emily B. Lyle, and Katherine Campbell, and published by Mercat Press, which is based on the manuscript versions of the songs collected by Greig and Duncan in the early part of the twentieth century and held by Historic Collections in the University of Aberdeen.

Thanks for permissions for the use of the following published material:

Harper Collins regarding material from *101 Scottish Songs* by Norman Buchan, Odyssey Productions o/b/o the Estate of Alan Lomax for material from *Singing in the Streets,* Conrad and Sue Wilson of Ramsay Head Press for material from *Murder Murder Polis*, Routledge and Kegan Paul per Thomson Publishing Services for material from *The Traditional and National Music of Scotland* and *Dae Ye Min' Langsyne?*

Permission to quote material from the School of Scottish Studies Archives is gratefully acknowledged.

I have sought to identify all my sources and to get permission to include any copyright material that is in quantity over the limits of general publishing practice. I apologise for any errors or omissions and would be grateful to learn of any necessary corrections.